Getting Started with Middle School Chorus

Second Edition

Patrick K. Freer

Published in partnership with
MENC: The National Association for Music Education

ROWMAN & LITTLEFIELD EDUCATION
A division of
ROWMAN & LITTLEFIELD PUBLISHERS, INC.
Lanham • New York • Toronto • Plymouth, UK

Published in partnership with MENC: The National Association for Music Education

Published by Rowman & Littlefield Education
A division of Rowman & Littlefield Publishers, Inc.
A wholly owned subsidary of The Rowman & Littlefield Publishing Group, Inc.
4501 Forbes Boulevard, Suite 200, Lanham, Maryland 20706
http://www.rowmaneducation.com

Estover Road, Plymouth PL6 7PY, United Kingdom

British Library Cataloguing in Publication Information Available

Library of Congress Cataloging-in-Publication Data

Freer, Patrick K.
  Getting started with middle school chorus / Patrick K. Freer. — 2nd ed.
      p. cm.
  "Published in partnership with MENC, The National Association for Music Education."
  ISBN 978-1-60709-163-9 (pbk. : alk. paper) — ISBN 978-1-60709-164-6 (electronic)
  1. Choral singing—Instruction and study—Juvenile. 2. School music—Instruction and study. I. MENC, the National Association for Music Education (U.S.) II. Title.
  MT915.F75 2009
  782.5071'2—dc22   2009014427

∞ ™ The paper used in this publication meets the minimum requirements of American National Standard for Information Sciences—Permanence of Paper for Printed Library Materials, ANSI/NISO Z39.48-1992.

Printed in the United States of America

Contents

Introduction

Welcome to the challenge of middle school choir! Whether you are embarking on the first teaching position of your career, are moving to your first experience with young adolescents, or are an experienced teacher looking for new ideas regarding scheduling, recruitment, or choral literature, this book aims to address your needs. It does not encompass every situation or every need, nor does it provide every answer to every question. These chapters contain proven solutions to situations that frequently face teachers at the middle school level.

This book is intended to help you address the needs of the great majority of students who are capable of participating in a choral program and who need little or no adaptation for special circumstances or learning abilities. As a middle school teacher, however, you may experience the joys and complications of working with students who face an array of cognitive, social, and physical challenges. You will help these students most when you focus on their abilities rather than their deficits.

Occasionally you will need to adjust your lessons and expectations to incorporate the needs of a specific student or group of students. Seek the advice and knowledge of other teachers and the school's support staff, where needed.

As a beginning teacher, you are undertaking a quest for success. Attaining success can give you the courage to experiment with unfamiliar choral repertoire or to try a new teaching technique. With a little effort, you can soon achieve success. Remember that your success as a teacher depends on the success of your students, both individually as young musicians and collectively as a choral ensemble. Take time to notice lessons or moments in rehearsal that are especially effective, and try to build on that foundation in subsequent days. Maintain open communication with your principal, support staff, parents, and colleagues. They will be able to celebrate your successes and help guide you toward continued achievement.

Many beginning teachers become so overwhelmed by duties and responsibilities that they forget to engage in personal music making. Do everything you can to make music for yourself and with others. Try not to lose the opportunity to participate in an adult choir or some other musical activity. These experiences can help refresh you at the end of a long day and spark new ideas for future classes you may teach.

One thing that we know about young adolescents is their need for interaction with others. These middle school students need opportunities for both individual and collective music making, especially when they feel like their teachers are co-musicians with them rather than "directors." That is why the term "choral teachers" is utilized in this book instead of terms like "choral directors" or "choral conductors." Many choral teachers in my area have name badges that read "Director of Choral Activities." Is that all? Maybe you do direct the activities of a choir, but you are, firstly and most importantly, a teacher—a choral music teacher. Directing or conducting a choir isn't even possible without students who know something about music. Your job is to lead, to inspire, to be musical—to teach.

Seek the same success in your students that you demand of yourself. Aim high, and don't be afraid to ask for help.

Chapter One

In the Beginning

Congratulations! You've just hung up the phone after being told you're the new choral director at Lowell Mason Middle School. What now?

If you're anything like the typical middle school student you've just been assigned to teach, you probably have more energy at this moment than you can contain. After all, you have a job—a good job—in the field you love. The next few months will see you channel that energy in many different directions. You will need to decide which directions to pursue, which can wait, and which you'll eventually decide to abandon altogether. Now is the time to get started.

THE MIDDLE SCHOOL TODAY

Before the 1970s, the junior high school reigned supreme in intermediate education. Grades 7–9 were structured completely differently from elementary education. Junior high school was similar to the high school model, where each student moved from classroom to classroom, responsible for his or her own acquisition of knowledge and skills. Students in junior high choral music programs experienced repertoire and performance opportunities made attainable because of the relative maturity of ninth grade voices. Owing to the range in students' ages, junior high choirs not only had male students with changing voices, but also many boys who could sing the lowest parts of SATB music.

Things changed with the establishment of middle schools. These schools grew to be communities of exploration where students could experiment with many different courses and activities. Ideally, middle schools encourage and celebrate the best of each student rather than high-light the accomplishments of only the brightest or most talented students. Middle school is a place for inquiry, with teachers serving as facilitators for finding information rather than functioning as exclusive sources of information. Middle school choral teachers today can use repertoire as the focal point of a wide range of music-related activities including music lit-eracy, vocal production, music history, composition, and improvisation.

DEVELOPING A FOCUS

One of the first things you'll be faced with is determining the focus of your program. Although some school administrators might want their school's choral program to be the largest in the state, the winner of blue ribbons at festivals and contests, a training ground for musical theatre pro-duction, or capable of performing concerts in multiple foreign languages, those ideas aren't always possible or even desirable in reality.

Middle school choral directors are always struggling to define the ap-propriate ratio of easily accessible music to more sophisticated music from the traditional choral repertoire. Some teachers decide that, since it could initially be easier to attract the attention of students with popular music and show tunes, that type of repertoire will be the focus of their programs. Other music teachers are faced with students coming from elementary school choral programs that explored many cultures through a significant number of musical styles. With emphasis on meeting state and national standards for music education, some teachers decide that a challenging, varied repertoire must be their focus. Still others continually reevaluate their programs for the best balance between the easily ac-cessible and the challenging, and some don't think about the balance of repertoire much at all.

When you develop your plans for the middle school choral program you have just begun to lead, you need to examine your school, your edu-cational philosophy, and your long-range goals. You may not be able to resolve these issues until you've been teaching a year or so. You may also find that your answers change over time. Very early in the school year, eager parents and students will want to know your plans for the year and perhaps your plans for the future direction of the choral program. It will be important for you to be able to articulate your current ideas, remembering that even "I won't know for sure until I've experienced my first year" is a great answer. There is nothing more highly prized than honesty.

DEVELOPING EXPECTATIONS

Once you have a good idea of what you want to develop in the areas of performance and student musical achievement, you will constantly find yourself adjusting your lessons to make them more accurately align with those goals. You will know if you're achieving your goals as you monitor your students' musical growth. The way to measure that growth is to establish expectations for student successes.

Your primary job is to give students the tools to master the singing of choral music. For example:

- If you expect students to read music, you will teach them how to read music notation.
- If you expect students to sing with a free, clear tone quality, you will teach them how to produce that sound physically.
- If you expect students to be able to practice independently, you will teach them the necessary skills and encourage them to establish their own practice times.
- If you expect students to work in groups, you will teach them cooperative learning skills.

Always keep your broad goals in mind as you begin the work of teaching individual lessons and conducting individual rehearsals. And remember that at least some of your students may not have had any musical training before your arrival in the school. Every step toward achieving goals should be celebrated—by both you and your students.

HAVING THE RIGHT ATTITUDE

Look around at your school's faculty during the first staff meeting of the year. Which teachers look as if they're having fun? Which ones look like they'd rather be back at the beach or vacationing in the mountains? Which ones look like they can't wait to get into the classroom? Which teachers seem approachable? Trustworthy? Likable? Competent? How can you tell? You may remember that a first impression is usually a correct impression. The best teachers in your school are probably easily identifiable without your speaking to them. The first impression can reveal a lot.

The first impression you give your fellow teachers stays with them for a long time, too. If you enter your teaching career, especially at the middle school level, without a sense of humor, the ability to be flexible, and the willingness to compromise, you'll spend many days pondering what went wrong. Humor, flexibility, and compromise are three of the most valuable attributes of effective middle school teachers. None of these characteristics in any way signals that you don't take your job seriously or that you haven't set high expectations for yourself and your students. What they do signal is that you're approachable and willing to work cooperatively.

Your administrators, fellow teachers, students, and parents need you to be approachable. Set your standards for curriculum and conduct; however, be open to change based on new information or experiences. Remain consistent, calm, and dignified. Avoid implying that you may know how to do things better than another, more experienced teacher. Your job is to work hard, laugh easily, and make outstanding music.

WHAT NEXT?

Now that you've got the job and are beginning to plan for the future, don't be surprised if these questions run through your mind in the next few days or weeks:

- "How should I run my rehearsals?"
- "If I've got unchanged and changing voices in the same room, what music should I choose?"
- "What can I expect from an unauditioned choir?"
- "Why does Nick just get up and walk around the room?"
- "Is there a way I can take all of this energy and create something musical?"
- "What should I teach in general music, and what should I teach in choir?"

- "How can I teach to a middle school philosophy while ensuring that the students are becoming ready for the high school choral experience?"
- "Are there national or state standards I should be implementing?"
- "Am I supposed to be a friend to these students?"
- "Will what I do during rehearsal today make it more likely—or less likely—that my students will be singing in choirs twenty years from now?"
- "How can I make this as much fun as I thought it would be?"

Onward . . .

Chapter Two

Your School's Choral Program

When you become the choral music teacher at a middle school, your role can be compared to that of a parent. No matter what you dreamed of in years past, one day you'll wake up to find that you've got a family of choirs, each with its own particular history and quirks, each having distinct needs and desires, and each needing to be guided toward the next level of development. In a functioning family, a parent is a leader who provides stability for each child in the family. A well-functioning choral program also sees its teacher as a leader, with each choir developing, growing, and performing independently. Like a parent confidently leading children toward adulthood, but with shorter-term goals, the choral music teacher has a clear sense of how all of the choirs contribute to producing musicians ready for high school experiences.

Unfortunately, not all families function the way we hope. Families can be dysfunctional, each unit operating independently without a unifying purpose. Perhaps the "family" of choirs you have acquired needs some help. To build the kind of well-functioning choral family you envision, you'll need to look at the choirs that have existed in the past, those that have already been assigned to you, and those you'd like to see emerge in the future.

WHAT KIND OF ENSEMBLES DO I HAVE?

It is especially important in the first years of teaching to make the most of whatever situation you have inherited. Your school may have a legacy of specific choirs singing specific repertoires; a program where students sing while eating their hamburgers and fries; or choral groups configured exactly the opposite of what you believe to be best. One way of finding out the history of your school's choral music program is to review old concert programs, which are usually on file in the main office. You can also look at photos in recent school yearbooks or the choir's web page to get an idea of the types of ensembles and the number of students enrolled.

Unless you have a clear mandate and support from your new administration, it's perhaps best not to make major changes in the structure of the choral program until you've become established in the school. Once you have proven your strengths as a teacher and logistical wizard, the school community will more likely be receptive to your suggestions for change. A new teacher may find adding to the existing choral program easier than deleting longstanding ensembles or activities. For example, starting a new boys' choir is easier than eliminating an established girls' choir and replacing it with a mixed ensemble.

For now, focus on the ensembles that are already part of the school structure. You'll have many years to develop your school's program into one that more closely matches your vision of the ideal choral program.

WHAT KIND OF ENSEMBLES DO I WANT?

Perhaps you're facing a choral program in need of immediate assistance in developing direction and focus. Whether you get to make changes right away or have to wait patiently for future years, it's important to have a sense of the direction in which you will eventually mold the program.

To Audition or Not?

Auditioned Ensembles

Many educators have strong opinions about auditioning. Teachers who favor auditioned ensembles feel that the audition gives them a chance to discover which students are truly interested in choral music, to meet and assess the strengths of each student, and to ensure that the choral ensembles are able to perform the chosen repertoire.

Open Enrollment Ensembles

Teachers who favor open enrollment believe that the middle school philosophy encourages all students to take risks by testing their abilities in a wide array of venues, one of which is choral music. These teachers generally dislike the notion of tacitly saying, "Kyle is good enough to participate in choral music, but Steve isn't." Imagine a seventh grader who summoned enough courage to audition for you, only to be told he or she wasn't good enough to participate. Would he or she ever sing for you again? Perhaps—but it's not likely.

Combinations

Many teachers arrive at a compromise in which some ensembles are auditioned and others are open to whoever can make the commitment of regular attendance and unwavering effort. This offers students who fail an audition the opportunity to improve their skills and try again when they feel fully prepared.

Voice Placement Hearings

Another idea is to listen to each student in your program, assessing him or her for pitch accuracy, rhythmic skills, music reading ability, and personality strengths. Middle school students are fascinated by discovering their capabilities, so be sure to share your findings with them and collaboratively plan strategies for them to experience even greater success. You can design an evaluation form based upon your own goals for this purpose. Use the voice placement hearing as a teaching tool that you and the student can use together to discover his or her current vocal range and other musical strengths or areas needing improvement. If used wisely, the voice placement hearing can allow you to assign students to the ensembles that they most accurately fit into while providing them with goals for future work that align with long-term classroom goals.

Types of Ensembles

What kinds of vocal ensembles exist in your vision of an ideal choral program? Here are some questions that you should think about when formulating this vision:

- Are the styles of music different for each group?
- Are the choirs multigrade or grade level choirs?
- Does the age of the students affect the repertoire chosen?
- Do the choral ensembles reflect the diversity of the student body?
- Should there be a traditional concert choir?
- Should there be a gospel choir?
- Will some of the choirs use movement and/or choreography in performance?
- Is there a show choir or vocal jazz ensemble?
- Are there both large and small ensembles?

If you find that some of the types of choral experiences mentioned here are unavailable to students at your school, you might want to think about steps you could take this year toward making those groups possible in the future.

Male and Female Choirs

Many middle school choral teachers find it helpful to separate girls from boys whenever possible. Sometimes dividing them means distinct boys' and girls' ensembles, and sometimes it can be accomplished by conducting sectional rehearsals with each gender. However achieved, there are certain advantages to having separate male and female ensembles. These include:

- Showing off for the opposite sex is eliminated.
- Students in gender-based ensembles face similar issues related to their physical and emotional development.
- The voice change process can be discussed frankly without fear of embarrassing the students. Boys tend to prefer all-male ensembles, especially when the teacher stresses teamwork much like in a sport.
- Audiences love to hear and see separate male and female choirs.

Although separate male and female choirs are beneficial at the middle school level, providing students opportunities to work together on mixed voicing repertoire is also highly important. Otherwise, your students will not be exposed to a large segment of the choral literature. Combining your female and male choirs to perform some mixed literature is advantageous and desirable.

TYPICAL GRADE LEVEL STUDENT CHARACTERISTICS

Sixth Grade

Sixth grade students have mostly treble ranges, including the boys, who may begin showing obvious signs of voice change as they grow older during the school year. Adjusting to middle school can be a challenge for these students, since middle schools often allow students more choices and social settings than they may have ever encountered before. You will find that music is often an area of comfort for sixth graders who have enjoyed the singing games and group participation experiences of elementary school music classes.

Seventh Grade

Seventh grade students often begin the year as a treble ensemble, with the boys gradually (occasionally quickly) gaining access to the pitches just below middle C. By the spring term, you'll probably need three-part mixed repertoire, with some boys singing on each part. Be aware that the "three-part mixed" voicing designation is designed to present limited ranges in all voice parts—this may or may not be ideal for your students. Many choral teachers find that multipart music is better suited to the vocal diversity of students at this age. Physical and social awkwardness is common with seventh graders. They may appear confident and gregarious on the outside, but their changing bodies alternately fascinate and frighten them.

The music teacher's role is to provide a measure of stability for seventh graders. They will expect you to be firm and fair, yet immediately flexible when presented with the changing moods and vocal characteristics of early adolescence.

Eighth Grade

Eighth grade singers can challenge middle school choral music teachers. You won't know what kinds of voices will show up from one day to the next, especially among your male singers. Be prepared to have multi-voice repertoire available, including SATB music with limited ranges for the lower voices. Be careful, however, of repertoire that is pitched too low for upper voices, particularly for girls' voices—which are almost always sopranos (despite what they may claim!). Eighth graders are young adults preparing to emerge from childhood. Watch for and encourage the growth of reasoning skills, personality development, and decision making processes. In short, enjoy watching eighth graders mature toward adulthood throughout the school year.

GENERAL MUSIC AND THE CHORAL REHEARSAL

Your school's general music classes can serve as excellent sources for skill development among your choral students. If these classes are scheduled throughout the entire academic year, then you have the chance to weave together common goals and skills with the choral rehearsal lesson plans. Frequently, however, choral ensembles function throughout an academic year, while general music classes last only a few weeks. In such a situation, choral ensembles should be structured to enhance and emphasize the information and skills gained during general music experiences. By incorporating singing into the general music experience, some students who might not have previously identified themselves as singers may gain an interest in your choral program.

GRADING

For some choral teachers, grading used to be easy—a simple comment such as "Nice voice" sufficed. Giving a class straight A's was sometimes the norm, and grading individual vocal performance was totally unexpected. The ground rules have changed. Measurement and evaluation can be some of our strongest, most effective teaching tools. Music teachers should give grades for each singer's ability to demonstrate vocal skills in the rehearsal and, where appropriate, in the general music classroom.

We need to construct each evaluative procedure as a learning tool, providing specific feedback to the student so that plans for continued improvement can be devised. Nearly all research throughout education is promoting "authentic assessment," that is, measurements that provide distinct criteria by which teachers can objectively evaluate student ability and progress—including skills in vocal music. For instance, authentic assessment could include opportunities for students to demonstrate their knowledge of dynamics by singing a familiar melody that you have edited to include various markings of musical expression.

School Policy and Past Precedent

Your school probably has a grading policy for the arts program. Ask about this policy before the first day of class. Some students will surely ask you how you grade, and this information should be presented up front as a part of beginning class or school and included in any syllabus or choral handbook. Whatever the school policy on grading, be ready to answer by presenting the list of criteria upon which you will base your grades for the marking period. If you find that your school does not issue grades for choral ensembles, you may wish to have students complete periodic voice placement hearings as described previously on page 11. If they receive some form of evaluation, students are held accountable for their own musical development regardless of any grade they may receive.

Objective and Subjective Grading

One way to evaluate student progress is by having the student complete a task (such as a multiple choice test, identification of pitch names, or clapping out a rhythm) and then objectively giving him or her a grade. Another way to measure knowledge and skills is by means of another individual's judgment, usually the teacher's. This is called subjective grading, and the grader uses phrases such as "in my opinion" or "I think" during the grading process.

Managing the Grading Process

You are probably assigned at least several hundred students to teach each academic year in your school—more students than any teacher except perhaps the physical education teacher. How on earth do you manage to give fair and accurate grades for each student? An obvious solution is to simply give each student a grade at the end of each marking period (or semester) based on how you feel he or she did. The problem with this type of grading system is that, while there may be some accountability required from the student, a subjective grade is usually influenced by individual student behaviors manifested in social settings such as choral rehearsals. While some schools issue grades for student behavior, most encourage teachers to evaluate students directly on their demonstration of knowledge and skills.

A better solution would be to assign grades based upon specific criteria. One suggestion is that you schedule a grade for each individual class session, choosing from a variety of grading formats and criteria. You might announce to the class, "Today's grade will be based on. . . ." You can complete the sentence using criteria such as recognition of rhythmic patterns, sight-reading skills, historical knowledge of the repertoire, singing the correct notes, and skills and knowledge from a multitude of other areas. Then, you need to focus on that one issue for the purposes of grading for that day.

There are many different ways you can expand the accuracy and meaningfulness of your grading system. Consult textbooks, MENC resources, and other professional improvement materials when investigating the following topics related to evaluating student progress:

- portfolio assessment of choral students
- computer-assisted grading programs
- rating scales and rubrics for specific skills

By the end of a semester, you will undoubtedly have many grades for each student that reveal trends in his or her strengths and weaknesses. This is especially helpful when parents question your grading methods or ask about ways in which their child can improve upon his or her grade (or become a stronger musician). Multiple grades can present an accurate measure of learning because students have been provided multiple opportunities to perform at their maximum levels.

All teachers, but especially first year teachers, should be prepared to share their grading procedures with parents, administrators, and students whenever the question arises. This sharing will facilitate open lines of communication among all who are involved in the education of your students.

The following is a suggested but not exhaustive list of knowledge and skills that you might evaluate:

- pitch accuracy
- rhythmic accuracy
- expressive qualities (dynamics, phrasing)
- articulation of vowels and consonants
- performing posture
- preparation for class (homework and materials)
- musical terminology encountered in octavos
- historical or cultural background of repertoire selections
- biographical information about composers

Note that each of these areas can be evaluated using many methods, including but not limited to:

- teacher grade
- written quiz
- student self-grade
- student evaluation of other students
- student audio recording and self-evaluation of singing

Final Thoughts about Grading

Remember to take special care with any scoring method, since adolescents often confuse criticism of vocal skills with criticism of themselves. Perhaps we should all keep that distinction very clear in our teaching and in our lives as singers. A setback or limitation in one area is not a failure—it only defines an area that may need work. Develop your evaluation procedures to ensure that students come to view assessment as a barometer of success, a road map for future work, and a challenge to grow and learn.

Chapter Three

Budget and Equipment

Take a look at the classroom you have inherited. If you're lucky, you have your own classroom with state-of-the-art equipment, from lightweight choral risers to MIDI-equipped computers, a Smart Board, an LCD projector, wireless internet access, and high quality video/audio recording equipment. If you're sort of lucky, you have your own classroom with some supplies, a piano, a good boombox, and a computer. If you're unlucky, you have some equipment and supplies, but no place to call your own. You travel from classroom to classroom for general music classes but hold choral rehearsals on the stage. Maybe gym classes or cafeteria lunches are in session just inches from your rehearsals, but at least your performers have a place to sing. If you're very unlucky, everything you have is on your "class on a cart," and sometimes you end up teaching in the hallway, locker room, or cafeteria, before or after school.

No matter which position you find yourself in, any situation can be improved with some creative spending, even on a limited budget. Having a little leeway in your budget may not allow you to change where you teach, but it certainly can make your job easier and more enjoyable—if you are reasonably savvy about it.

MAKE A WISH LIST

In many school systems, projecting budgets begins extraordinarily early. One of the first surprises for many new teachers is the task of making budget projections for the following academic year. Your first budget-related task should be to develop a wish list of what to purchase a year or more ahead. This list is usually the basis for estimating next year's actual budget request, which you will submit a month or so into the current school year. Aim high, but keep your proposals realistic. Let the budget developers and decision makers know exactly what you need to create a first-rate program, even it if means submitting the same items many years in a row because they are eliminated annually.

Begin collecting catalogs as soon as you find out you have a teaching assignment. If you're not on the mailing lists of music supply companies, publishers, and professional resource outlets, call to request current catalogs. You will need them almost right away to help you create your first wish list. Though much of this information is available on the internet, printed catalogs help some teachers visualize their needs more easily.

The Well-Equipped Choral Classroom

A solid program requires specific equipment so that a music educator can maximize the effect of his or her teaching and mount successful student performances. Take an inventory of what your school has and what it is lacking. If you're a new teacher coming into the classroom during the summer months, ask another teacher or administrator if some equipment you had expected to see is shared between classrooms or stored in another location (which may explain why it's missing from your room!).

A complete audio-visual system can be expensive, but it is well worth researching and building over a period of two or three years. Get good quality CD recording and duplication equipment as soon as you can.

Other important audio-visual equipment includes DVD players, LCD projectors, and quality audio speakers. For playback in the classroom, make certain that equipment is compatible with any MP3 players you may use to organize your daily listening excerpts. These and other items are presented in the checklist below, but the checklist is offered with the full acknowledgement that the definition of *state of the art* changes very rapidly with respect to technology. Don't sacrifice quality equipment for the latest gadgets, but don't be afraid to change with the times, either.

Checklist: Audio-Visual System Requirements

The following checklist is provided to get you thinking of audio-visual equipment that might be included in your budget requests.

_____ television and DVD player/recorder (and VCR if needed)

_____ good quality CD recording and duplication equipment

_____ Smart Board (or equivalent)

_____ LCD projector

_____ digital video recording equipment

_____ digital audio recording equipment, configured for "in the moment" recordings of in-progress rehearsals

_____ CD player system and quality speakers (check compatibility with MP3 players)

_____ portable cassette tape recorders (for quick student projects and assessment)

_____ ample electrical outlets

_____ computers for teacher and students

_____ keyboards with full-sized keys and headphones

BUDGETING FOR PERFORMANCES

The list of equipment required for a single performance (see the Performance Needs checklist on page 22) is deceptively simple. However, the logistical issues involved in dealing with performance equipment can be challenging. You need specifics about where your concert will take place, whether it is a school auditorium, a local church, a park, or someplace else, so that you can evaluate what equipment is required. Risers may or may not be supplied; if not, they must be brought from school or borrowed from another school or a community choir. Accompaniment is usually an issue, unless the students will be singing a cappella. If a piano will be used, you need to find out if it is of sufficient quality to support the performance. If it is a school piano, tuning and repair need to be planned for in the budget. Piano moving expenses may also need to be planned for—although you should first find out if the piano fits through the doorways of wherever you need it to go (I write this from personal experience!). An electronic or battery-powered keyboard may prove more feasible, and that is also a budget item. If you are performing multicultural/world, holiday, or other special event music, percussion may be required. Some expense may be spared if percussion is available from your school's instrumental program.

You may also need an easily portable podium for conducting performances that will take place away from school. Many hardware stores carry stepstool/toolbox combinations made of durable plastic that are great for rehearsals or off-campus performances. (They are also useful for storing spare music on the road.)

Transportation must also be paid for. Bus rental fees may come out of the music budget or a general school fund. Ask what teachers did in the past, and keep track of the amount spent for each concert.

Checklist: Performance Needs

Be sure you know the financial procedures related to the following items before you commit your choir to specific performances:

_____ performance venue
_____ piano
_____ risers
_____ transportation
_____ sound system/amplification system
_____ conductor's podium
_____ electronic keyboard
_____ percussion equipment

. . . and don't forget about obtaining formal administrative approval and necessary parental permission slips for any performances!

FREQUENTLY OVERLOOKED BUDGET ITEMS

There will be many times during the year when you will find yourself saying something like, "How in the world did I forget to order chalk and dry erase markers?" Use the list below to help you remember some of the items you might have forgotten, and write additional items in the margins as you think of them.

Checklist: Did You Remember to Order These?

_____ music octavos
_____ instrumentalist and accompanist fees
_____ concert programs, publicity, and tickets
_____ piano tuning
_____ registration fees for field trips and/or competitions
_____ audition and participation fees for students in honor choirs
_____ professional development (conventions, workshops, courses)
_____ choir uniforms
_____ conductor's podium
_____ classroom supplies
_____ audio and visual cassette tapes, recordable CDs and DVDs
_____ batteries for keyboards and audio equipment
_____ power adapters for keyboards
_____ file folders for octavo storage and student record keeping
_____ concert folders
_____ pencils and erasers
_____ headphones for students (order extra for mid-year replacements)

THE BUDGET DEVELOPMENT PROCESS

Finding Out Who Develops the Budget

In most schools, teachers submit budget requests to either a principal or supervisor for approval. Your school may have a different process where the budget may be developed by committee, by department, or by the principal/supervisor. In these cases, use your wish list as a guide for deciding which items to include in your discussions and which ones to defer.

Determining the Availability of Funds

Find out at what point during the current school year funds for the next academic year become available. Assuming that the district budget is approved, it is a good idea to finalize your ordering before the end of the current year. School finance offices are invariably swamped with requests in the summer, often delaying order processing. Get your purchase orders into the appropriate office as soon as you can.

There is another reason for prompt submission of purchase orders. Many districts freeze budgets at a variable point during the academic year, depending upon when available funds for the district's basic operating expenses become low. Ask your principal, administrative assistant, or secretary about the approximate date the budget might freeze and become inaccessible during the school year. Make sure you have spent every cent of your budget long before that point. If not, your principal has every right to come to you with the statement, "Look, your budget for next year is smaller because you apparently didn't need all of the funds available to you this year." Use any surplus funds available to you to purchase items from your current wish list, or to order items you'll need during the first few weeks of the coming school year.

Ordering New Music

Check with your school's administration before purchasing new repertoire. Most schools have strict procedures that must be followed regarding the purchase of any materials. Shop around for the best price. Many large distributors offer substantial discounts off the list price of music octavos. You might even ask for advice from the choir director at the college you attended. Alumni working in the music industry often provide discounts to graduates of their alma maters. It never hurts to ask.

Generally, music education budget allocations are inadequate. If you just can't seem to make ends meet on the amount you're given, look carefully at your purchases of new choral music. There may be some pieces that students can share. For example, do you really need one hundred copies of the "Battle Hymn of the Republic" when you see your students only in groups of thirty?

If you have a friend teaching in another school who is also struggling with a tight choral budget, consider programming much of the same music for a year. You can each use half of the titles in the fall and then switch for the spring term. Also, investigate borrowing procedures for music at county and state music teachers' organizations. They can be a rich source of repertoire.

Planning Ahead

It will probably take your district's central office at least several weeks to process, order, and receive shipment of the pieces you order. Remember that your budget covers an entire year. Always leave a small amount of funds in your account for unexpected situations, but make certain to spend it just before the budget becomes frozen. If you find yourself with extra funds, begin to purchase for the following year. Additionally at this time, order some repertoire that you feel is essential to a quality library.

WHAT IF THERE'S *NO* BUDGET?

Yes, it sometimes happens that there is no budget for choir. Because veteran teachers have learned to submit their purchase orders before the end of the academic year, during your first year you may find yourself using whatever the former choral teacher ordered at the end of last year. Employing a few strategies to deal with this situation may ease your predicament.

It's not too early to discuss budget during the final interview process, but if you did not, ask the principal what the status of your budget is when you receive your teaching appointment. As part of this conversation, ask for copies of the previous year's purchase orders so that you can see what was ordered and when it is to be delivered. Look at the copies privately. If you decide the orders include items you do not want, ask your principal whom to contact to find out if it's still possible to substitute your own purchase orders for those already submitted. If you discover that you have no funds, then it's time to become creative.

Talk to the principal again, if necessary, to see if emergency funds can be appropriated for your use, even if they have to be deducted from the next academic year's budget. Ask your contacts in choral teaching to help you estimate the minimum you will actually need to achieve a successful teaching year.

When You Cannot Order New Music

If you find yourself with limited funds during the first year of your teaching, here are some strategies you may find useful in this situation:

- Use your school's library to the fullest extent possible.
- Use other libraries in the district.
- Ask the local college if you can borrow repertoire in exchange for the college's using one of your ensembles as a demonstration choir for music education methods classes.
- Arrange your favorite folk song for your sixth grade choir.
- Invent a unit on choral arranging for your choirs and then use the results of their creativity in a concert with student conductors.
- Introduce the theme-and-variations form to your students; then compose several variations on a familiar tune, including tempo, accompaniment, mode, and text. Songs like "Brother John" work well for this project.
- Work with the local college's composition class. A possible composition project may be having the class write for the specific requirements of your choir.
- Use choral music that is freely available for download from the Choral Public Domain Library (www.cpdl.org).
- Post a message on the appropriate bulletin board at www.choralnet .org requesting assistance from choral teachers across the country and beyond. Be sure to explore the hundreds of repertoire resources (many are free!) that are linked through this site.
- Consult with your local high school choral music teacher to determine if there is any appropriate literature in his or her library.

Additional Funding Sources

If your classroom lacks important pieces of equipment or essential materials, approach the school's Parent Teacher Association (PTA) for funds. Being visible and active in the PTA can also help if you should need funding or organizational support later on. Another possibility is a Music Parents Association (MPA) that raises funds and provides helping hands at choral events. Confer with experienced area music educators to evaluate whether starting an MPA is feasible. If creating an MPA seems premature, place a want ad in your school newspaper or parent newsletter for assistance and items that you need.

Just as the second edition of this book went to press, my hometown orchestra program found itself with no budget for instrument purchases. A plea for the donation of instruments was printed in the newspaper, and the result was a huge number of instruments in decent condition. Even better was the donation of repair services by local music store personnel. Again, it never hurts to ask!

When you are finally able to place your own orders, avoid the trap of ordering only choral music octavos. Include items for the classroom and your own teaching supplies in your purchase orders. Be kind to yourself. If you really need a stapler, buy a stapler with funds from your school budget. Resist the altruistic impulse of running out to the mall and purchasing items out of your own wallet.

No matter how carefully you plan for your budgetary needs, you will invariably find areas for improvement in future budgets: finding more reliable vendors, ordering those small but important items for your desk, or developing entirely new areas for future expenditures. Remember to keep a list of these items and update it faithfully throughout the year. And next year, when the budget development process begins anew, be sure that the items contained in your budget are placed there thoughtfully, helping you build toward the choral music program you envision.

Finally, remind yourself that the most important factor in good teaching is a good teacher, not an abundance of materials.

ONE FINAL CONSIDERATION ABOUT BUDGETING: THE PENCIL WARS

During your first year, you'll find yourself busy with important things like winning student respect, preparing for your first concert, and trying to stay ahead of the next demand on your time. Is it really worth the energy to argue with students about forgotten pencils or other common supplies? Plan the purchase of a few dozen pencils into your budget and devise a system for borrowing pencils and the like by asking for student collateral—a backpack, for example. It comes down to which battles you choose to fight. Nobody ever became a great teacher because his or her students brought pencils to class.

Chapter Four

Developing Your Schedule

To get an idea of how your schedule affects your teaching plans, look at two schedules: your daily teaching schedule and your performance schedule.

DAILY SCHEDULE

By now, you most likely know how many periods you teach each day and the length of each period. You should also have a general idea of how choir classes were scheduled in previous years. If you're fortunate, your choir rehearsal is scheduled during the academic day, and the school's master schedule limits demands on student time. In some schools, however, choir is offered only before or after school hours, during lunch, or as a "pull-out," meaning that students have to miss another class to come to choir. Sometimes choir is offered as a part of general music, and all general music students form a large ensemble. If so, teachers need to schedule extra rehearsals for the entire group.

You may be unable to change your first year schedule significantly. If you feel that the schedule you must follow is not meeting your needs or your students' needs adequately, join long range planning or site-based management committees to influence how future schedules are developed. Look closer. At first glance, it may seem as though the opportunities to meet with your choral students are somewhat limited. But for small group or ensemble rehearsals, your schedule is perhaps more flexible than you imagine.

Holding half-period rehearsals during your regularly scheduled general music classes is a possibility. For the first half of the period, general music students would have a lesson with you, and then they could work on a project or assignment while you rehearse choral students in another area of the room. Another option is rotating student rehearsals throughout the day, so that pull-out rehearsals affect other classes only once every few weeks. It may also be possible to share students with the instrumental teacher—either exchange students halfway through the period or alternate days between band and choir. Some school districts compensate teachers who work with students during non-teaching hours by providing a change in the teacher's daily schedule. Ask your principal about the possibility of allowing you to either arrive at school later or leave earlier on days you give extra rehearsals during your preparation or lunch periods.

Another way of dealing with scheduling problems might be to establish "learning stations" throughout the room at which you have choral sections rehearse independently. With an electronic keyboard and audio/visual equipment at each station, students could follow your recorded lesson or record and analyze their own work. With four-part repertoire, this option could quadruple the effectiveness of your rehearsal time.

A Caution about Pull-Out Rehearsals

A common problem for busy middle school students arises when there is a pull-out schedule for the choral program, meaning that students need to miss a regularly scheduled class for a rehearsal. This often requires extra work for the student, since any missed classwork will eventually need to be completed. Pull-out music schedules are of greater concern when they juxtapose a choir rehearsal with an exam, project, or classroom activity that is important to the student.

Unfortunately, occasions may arise when a classroom teacher either is unable or simply refuses to allow the student to attend the choral rehearsal. Such situations need to be resolved between the teachers, not by holding the student responsible for a situation he or she did not create. Remain aware of your position as a role model in these types of situations. Students need to see you handle such problems with tact and maturity.

MANAGING TIME AS A PROFESSIONAL

Music teachers' days are demanding, but a good teacher still needs time to reflect upon what has happened in a particular day's lessons or rehearsals and plan ways to improve. If you are always busy, your well-intentioned activity can result in a downward spiral toward mediocrity as you run out of time to plan effective lessons, or even to get enough sleep. Remember that you're a role model for students, and that includes how you handle your time.

Music teachers often stand all day, use their voices constantly, conduct extra rehearsals before and after school, give extra help during lunch, and have their own professional performing careers. Before you say "yes" to extra projects, such as a pep chorus for basketball games or a show choir, ask yourself if you can truly give 100 percent to each of them. If not, select a fewer number of projects with which you can be successful.

PERFORMANCE SCHEDULE

During the school year, your choirs will be expected to sing at a variety of events. These may include school assemblies, district-wide concerts, off-campus performances, or performances in other venues. While they share much in common, each of these events has its own characteristics. Careful timing of performances can maximize your choir's learning experience by giving you an opportunity to prepare them to perform at their highest level of achievement.

Scheduling Concerts

Inquire about the concert schedule as soon as you arrive at your school. Find out if the concert schedule has already been set and publicized and if there are any traditional or preferred times of the year for concerts. Perhaps some performance dates could be changed if necessary, or the principal may have scheduling preferences. Ask about the location of each performance and if an instrumental program must be coordinated in the planning. Find out the facilities' schedules and when they can be reserved. Either continue or establish an attendance policy for choral students at concerts. But be sure to do this in collaboration with the school administration because many schools have already developed attendance/grading policies for events that take place beyond the daily schedule.

Honoring Tradition

Many schools have a tradition of choral performances that you will be obliged to honor, at least until you are established in the school and community. Often this tradition is embodied in concerts that take place at certain times of the year, in locations that have been used for years, with themes, religious significance, or social importance deeply ingrained in the community. Evaluate the repertoire that was performed in recent years at your school's performances. Regardless of your preferences, there may be extreme loyalty among students and parents toward specific styles and titles of music. Determine if there are any traditions, such as singing a particular piece with all choir alumni at the final concert of the year.

If you decide to alter the music that your students will study, remember to make changes gradually. You may need to mix some of the old with the new for a few years until you arrive at the repertoire balance you prefer. By then, your preferences may have become the established tradition.

School Assembly Programs

If choir performances at school assemblies are expected, ask your principal about holding a choir assembly in the spring rather than the fall. A later performance date gives you time to develop a solid rapport with your students and ensure that they are presenting only the most well-prepared material for the student body. Also, this will give you an idea of general student behavior in other assembly settings.

Assembly programs need to be positive experiences for both performers and audience members. By observing student behavior at other assemblies through the year, you will likely gain insights into how to structure and present your program in a way that will engage all participants. This will maximize the opportunity for a successful assembly experience.

Off-Campus Performances

Before mid-November, when requests from the community for concerts, recitals, and other choral performances start flooding your school mailbox, discuss the topic of off-campus performances with your principal. Decide which performance opportunities you will accept, such as at shopping malls, the local Rotary Club, nursing homes, or hospitals. If you choose to participate in off-campus performances, a few logistical issues regarding students need to be resolved, including transportation and how it is paid for, permission slips, medical forms, and meal arrangements. Well in advance of your trip, the school faculty will need a list of participating students to excuse them from classes. Finally, you will want to know if your school can accept monetary donations to the music program from groups for which you sing.

A Happier New Year

Many middle schools are moving away from December concerts in favor of January performances. These concerts can solve several problems posed by December concerts. Any holiday music included will seem less parochial in January, and students will not have to start rehearsing such repertoire so far in advance of the season. January is closer to the midpoint of most school calendars, which allows for a natural change in repertoire and schedules. Because some students may drop out of choral ensembles after a holiday concert, especially if a vacation follows immediately, a January concert can provide continuity across the winter recess.

Discuss your winter concert planning with school administrators. With a later concert, you may not need to be as exacting about programming music to reflect every cultural holiday viewpoint in your community. However, a part of your job is to reflect many of the surrounding community's values and traditions, and it is possible to do that without focusing exclusively on holiday selections. If you work in an area of the country that encourages religious holiday music in the schools, you need to weigh the pros and cons of various concert schedules and choose repertoire accordingly. Be sure to consult MENC's position statement on the use of sacred music in schools, available freely at www.menc.org/about/view/sacred -music-in-schools.

Festival Concerts

Festival concerts can be wonderful, especially for beginning teachers. These events usually encourage the presentation of a sample of your choir's most successful repertoire, give you a chance to meet other choral music teachers, and allow your students to observe others engaged in the art of choral music. Presented with other choirs in the school district, another middle school's choir, or a consortium of singing ensembles, festivals can be held annually. They can be related to a theme or tied to a particular celebration in your community, such as the opening of a new city hall facility or a new school.

Most festivals require no more than three numbers per ensemble and a final number with all of the singers combined. Teachers can present their choirs at their best, with the bonus of being seen and heard by large numbers of people who might not otherwise attend school concerts. Festivals are great opportunities to showcase the best of your ensemble's work while exposing the students to the pleasure of singing for other musicians.

Spring Concert Dates

A common dilemma for middle school choral music teachers occurs with scheduling concerts in the spring semester. If your concerts are scheduled only two months apart, for example in March and May, the number of rehearsals available to you for the second concert is quite limited. Your choir might not have enough time to learn a different repertoire well for the later concert. A way of dealing with this situation is to collaborate on a festival or other less stressful performance with another school for the earlier date. A performance featuring multiple choirs or a Music in Our Schools Month district-wide concert may relieve some of the pressure. If your choir sings only two pieces at the earlier performance, no one will mind if you use those pieces again as part of a larger concert two months later.

Only tradition obliges your choir to sing completely different music at every concert. There is a good deal of merit in selecting a challenge piece for your students that may require months of preparation. Consider asking the audience to notice improvements or changes in the performance of a piece that they hear more than once during the year. You might point out focus areas of recent rehearsals or describe what goals you have for upcoming rehearsals. Better yet, have students share that information as they introduce the repertoire during a concert.

AFTER THE FINAL CONCERT

After the final performance of the concert season, many teachers turn their choir rehearsals into class voice lessons by using time remaining in the school year to focus on solos and small ensembles. Student accomplishments resulting from these extra activities might be followed by a student recital or cabaret performance for invited guests. The final weeks of school also offer the flexibility to incorporate a higher concentration of music literacy, sight-singing, or even student conducting activities into your lessons. Many successful choral music teachers plan ahead and use this time to introduce repertoire for the coming fall semester.

Chapter Five

Finding and Choosing Choral Repertoire

Ask any choral educator about the most arduous task he or she faces, and the answer will almost surely be "choosing repertoire." Choral repertoire is the textbook of choral music education. Music educators use it to help students explore and develop vocal technique, make relationships between audible sounds and written notation, and discover the meaning of musicianship. Choosing music appropriate for adolescent voices is not easy. Compared to the vast quantities of literature written for treble choirs or high school ensembles, music specifically composed for middle school singers' voices is quite limited. Various music publishers and composers have embarked on ambitious projects to remedy this situation recently, but it is still difficult to find pieces that are not bowdlerized versions of repertoire originally written for other ensembles.

There are, however, a number of reliable sources. These include other schools' choral libraries as well as your own, colleagues in music education, and commercial vendors. Because discovering what you have might involve organizing it first, you should find out how to set up your choral library if you don't already have the know-how.

ORGANIZING YOUR SCHOOL'S LIBRARY

Imagine that you have unearthed and dusted off the choral library, expecting that the former teacher left everything sorted, marked, and cataloged. If you find chaos instead, you'll need to organize the library.

Whether you have a computerized database or not, you can spend exhausting amounts of time at this task. Here is a simple system that can be used successfully: All you need to do is assign each title a number. Sure, it might be helpful if you did some presorting and organized pieces by title, composer, or subject. Sooner or later, though, you will add pieces to the library, and you will be forever shuffling stacks of music around to make them fit. By assigning a number to each title and then keeping your music in filing cabinets or closets in numerical order, you will always know exactly where each piece is located.

After assigning a number, you can then use a computer database or index card filing system to keep track of the title, the composer/ arranger, the text author, the musical style (art song, jazz, American folk, holiday, and so on), the level of difficulty, the number of copies in the library, and when and where the piece was performed. The beauty of this system is that you can put your index card files or computer database into a thousand configurations—and you'll never misplace anything because each piece has just one number in your catalog. If you accidentally lose cards 1–10 of your index file, your backup is to open your closet door and see what pieces of literature belong to numbers 1–10. Simple. If you ever want to discard a piece of music from the library, you have only opened up a space and number for the next piece of music you buy.

Dealing with Outdated Music

Once you familiarize yourself with your library holdings, you can decide what is to be tossed and what will be kept in the files. If there is extra storage space, keep as much music as practical in your library. Throw away photocopied music. It's almost always illegal (see the next section, "A Quick Note about Copyright"). Discard music that is tied to a particular time or event and will never be performed again, for instance, "Disco: The Tender Moments" or "Kermit Salutes President Ford." However, double-check with your administration before discarding music and keep any music that might be valuable to another teacher. There may be a reason that the music has remained in your classroom for all of those years. If you have reason to believe that the music may be of historical significance to your school, archiving it may be the best approach. The school may have a location for archival materials, or the district may have a system for dealing with them.

A QUICK NOTE ABOUT COPYRIGHT

Music educators need to familiarize themselves with copyright restrictions and remain aware of any changes that occur because of developments in technology and electronic file sharing. There are two MENC resource web pages that are of particular assistance. First, the MENC Copyright Center contains an annotated listing of resources that may be critical when you face specific copyright questions or problems: www.menc.org/resources/view/copyright-center. The second resource is MENC's web page summarizing the main points of current copyright law: www.menc.org/resources/view/copyright-law-what-music-teachers-need-to-know.

No matter the information maintained by MENC, however, you are responsible for knowing the implications of copyright law and your responsibilities under the law. Plus, obeying copyright law helps ensure that composers and publishers are able to continue providing you with the music you use on a daily basis.

DETERMINING QUALITY IN CHORAL REPERTOIRE

One dilemma for new teachers is the selection of music for the choirs. Assuming that you know the ranges of your students and have a basic idea of their musical capabilities, coupled with your plans for teaching them knowledge and skills during the next few months, how do you choose from the many pieces which remain as options? Various teachers and conductors have offered advice on the selection of choral repertoire, often within the pages of the *Music Educators Journal* and the *Choral Journal*. This advice can often be reduced to key criteria against which you will evaluate the repertoire options. One of my favorite lists is now more than eighty years old, but I find it appealingly practical for today. Mabelle Glenn, an early president of MENC, offered this list in a 1928 article titled "A New Goal in Ensemble Singing":

> These are questions which I, as director of school choruses and a church choir, ask myself when choosing song material:
>
> 1. Is this poem worthy of a place in song literature?
> 2. Is there a well defined highest point in the song where there is opportunity for a significant climax?

3. Does this song offer an opportunity for a wide range of dynamics?
4. Is there a good swing? Whether slow or fast is there a decided rhythmic pulse?
5. Is there something of interest from the beginning to the end?
6. When the melody ceases to be the important element, is there something else to hold the interest of the listeners? (All too often one finds great portions that could be omitted without any loss.)
7. Is this selection well proportioned from an emotional standpoint? For example, is a highly dramatic passage balanced by a quiet passage?
8. Which word or words in each phrase are most important?
9. Which words are most capable of bringing beauty to the tone?
10. Which words have tone-cramping vowels and difficult consonants which will need special attention?
11. Do I have sufficient faith in this selection to give it a meaningful interpretation? (*Music Supervisors' Journal, 15*[1]: 67, 69, 71)

A more recent list is contained in the following chapter: "Meeting National Standards for Music Education through Choral Performance," by F. Abrahams in *Teaching Music through Performance in Choir*, volume 1, pages 57–79 (edited by H. J. Buchanan & M. W. Mehaffey, Chicago: GIA Publications, 2005).

The entire list is too lengthy to reprint here, but two of the most intriguing criteria for the selection of quality choral repertoire are:

1. The composition is consistent in its style, reflecting a complete grasp of technical details (including the vocal issues connected to the setting of text), and it avoids lapses into trivial, futile, or unsuitable passages.
2. The composition reflects a musical validity that transcends factors of historical importance or pedagogical usefulness.

That second point, the one about transcending pedagogical usefulness, is very important. Choral repertoire chosen for young adolescents needs to be the very best that is available given the capabilities of the choir. Choral repertoire forms the basis for how we teach toward achieving our curriculum goals, but it is the repertoire that comes first. Follow a set of criteria to determine the quality level of each piece you consider. Doing so will assist you in finding repertoire that is artistically satisfying at the same time that it presents opportunities for teaching knowledge and skills to your students.

Local Choral Libraries

Your first step in locating music is to inquire about the existing choral library when you arrive at your new school and begin to prepare the classroom for the new year. Find out where the library is located and ask if there is any other music stored in other locations in the school building. Make a preliminary assessment of what is on hand.

Before deciding to purchase new music, explore the choral libraries of other schools in your district. Learning what is available saves money and hurried research later, and you will know exactly what materials can be borrowed and what may still be lacking before the first day of school.

Fellow Choral Music Educators

Locating new music to examine for purchase is an important, ongoing task. The quickest, most reliable way to locate classroom and concert literature is to consult with other music educators. Beyond that, the quest for quality repertoire is similar to a hunt for hidden treasures in the sense that there are numerous places to look.

Experienced Teachers

These are your best resources. Asking for help from them accomplishes several objectives. It gives you an opportunity to call and introduce yourself. It shows your interest in cooperating with them and provides you with a wealth of knowledge about current and standard repertoire.

Don't limit yourself to teachers in your district. Call teachers in neighboring districts, talk to your former college classmates, and use the resource people identified by professional organizations you belong to. You can always leave e-mail or phone messages at the schools of the teachers you wish to contact. To obtain telephone numbers or e-mail addresses of teachers you only know by reputation, check their school's website. If you know only the teacher's name, call the appropriate board of education for more information. If the board won't release information, try networking with teachers you can reach.

Teacher-Led Reading Sessions

These events, often organized by professional organizations or colleges, include a tested repertoire recommended by an experienced teacher. The usefulness of the reading sessions is up to you. At a session, note the date and name of the session participant from whom you received the piece at the top of each octavo you read. Discard immediately what you know you will never use, unless you have unlimited space in your choral library. Later on, if you find that a piece you obtained at a reading session some years previously has gone out of print, you may be able to contact the original clinician and borrow copies. Another possibility is to contact the publisher and request written permission to photocopy the music.

Professional Organizations

MENC: The National Association for Music Education and the American Choral Directors Association (ACDA) provide numerous resources to help you locate music. First, their journals periodically publish lists and descriptions of appropriate repertoire and resource materials. Keep copies of these lists in a file folder for easy reference (or keep them electronically, if possible). Second, both organizations sponsor numerous reading sessions of both new and recommended repertoire. The journals and reading sessions serve as important resources for finding choral music.

Other important resources that the professional organizations provide are middle school/junior high state chairpersons, who usually are selected because of their knowledge of the repertoire and adolescent vocal development. Contact members of your state MENC and ACDA boards to determine who their chairpersons are. Frequently, the contact information for committee or section chairs is listed in the state journals.

Updated Festival and Contest Lists

Some professional organizations publish lists of repertoire at varying intervals. For example, the New York State School Music Association (NYSSMA) publishes a triennial list of repertoire for almost every imaginable ensemble, complete with publisher information and level of difficulty ratings. The Texas Music Educators Association (TMEA) also publishes repertoire lists. Various other states have developed their own lists as well. Additionally, many books about adolescent choirs contain repertoire lists. Verify the availability of published works with music publishers or distributors before you decide to use a piece more than two or three years old.

Festival Repertoire and Recordings

Growing numbers of festivals and all-state choirs feature middle school students. If you have a teaching acquaintance in another state or region, ask for the repertoire lists of the festivals in their areas. Also, obtain recordings of festivals and all-states; they provide outstanding repertoire selections sung by exemplary middle school choirs.

Commercial Sources

Music Stores

Most large music stores regularly receive single copies of recent releases. Call ahead to determine that the resources exist, and then spend an afternoon browsing through repertoire. Ask to examine the packets on approval, which means that you can return what you don't want to buy.

Publishers

Some of your best contact people for new and innovative repertoire work in the music industry. While not all publishers are able to fulfill your requests, some are extraordinarily generous and helpful. Establishing relationships with them can be mutually beneficial. When you find a salesperson or company representative eager to offer assistance, remember the person's name and send him or her a thank you note.

Internet Resources

The technology available to music teachers continues to expand. Many publishers, state organizations, and knowledgeable individuals trade repertoire lists through e-mail and other online computer services. The numerous message boards existing on the World Wide Web can be located using search engines. Many choral publishers and distributors now include octavos and recordings on their websites, some of which are available for purchase and immediate download. The octavos and recordings posted on these websites may be abbreviated versions for demonstration purposes only, but they are invaluable resources available at all hours of the day and night.

Be sure to explore the many repertoire resources linked through the ChoralNet website: www.choralnet.org. And don't forget about the music that is freely available in public domain through the Choral Public Domain Library: www.cpdl.org.

BASICS OF CONCERT PROGRAMMING

There are many excellent resources for ideas about how to select the repertoire to present in a concert setting. Many of these resources also include in-depth information about planning, scheduling, and organizing various types of formal concerts, informal musical presentations, touring, and Broadway-style musicals. Some ideas follow below, but you should also consult any textbooks you used in college (choral methods class) and/or the following four sources:

Books

Brinson, B. (1996). *Choral music: Methods and materials.* Wadsworth Thompson. ISBN: 0-02-870311-1.

- Excellent section on programming for individual concerts; Brinson compares choosing concert repertoire to designing a multi-course dinner party—a great analogy!

Phillips, K. H. (2004). *Directing the choral music program.* Oxford University Press. ISBN: 0-190-513282-3.

- This is a comprehensive resource for helping choral teachers think ahead about all of the "what do I do when ___ happens?" There is also a thorough description of how the entire concert evening should unfold—not just your choir's portion.

Articles

Brunner, D. (2004). Choral music design and symmetry. *Music Educators Journal 80*(6), 46–49.

- This article has become required reading for anyone programming a choral concert. Readers get to peer inside the brain of this well-known composer/conductor as he designs a high school choral concert. You'll be able to easily transfer the principles to a middle school setting.

Zielinski, R. (2005). The performance pyramid: Building blocks for a successful choral performance. *Music Educators Journal 90*(1), 44–49.

- This article and the accompanying online resources (at www.menc .org) provide one of the most thorough descriptions of how to plan rehearsals leading toward a concert.

The Overall Concert

Remember that your audience will be attending the entire concert, not just the portions that your choirs sing. Keeping this in mind as you choose repertoire for concert performance will help you orchestrate the evening so that students and parents leave with feelings of pride and excitement—not sheer exhaustion!

The concert should last no longer than ninety minutes from start to finish—that's everything, including all performances, intermissions, announcements, and transitions between pieces and ensembles. Audiences filled with working parents simply cannot be expected to give more time in any one evening, especially since they will have been involved in getting their child ready for the concert and providing transportation to and from the venue.

The concert length must determine how many pieces will be performed. There is absolutely no reason (beyond tradition!) that all ensembles should perform every selection they have rehearsed in class. Use the concert to highlight only those pieces that best represent what students have been learning.

Consider having students introduce each piece by reading a prepared paragraph about the concepts and techniques unique to that piece. This will help audience members remember that choral music in schools is, firstly, about music education.

Another often-overlooked opportunity when programming school choral concerts is the presentation of the same piece of music on multiple concerts throughout the year. This works especially well for pieces that present significant challenges to the choir, perhaps because of complexity, language, or duration. Again, having students introduce the piece can remind audience members of what the choir was able to successfully perform at the last concert and inform them of the progress to be noticed in the current concert. Student introductions like these also lay the groundwork for conversations in the car after the concert that go beyond "I really liked that piece!" and engage everyone in more substantive discussions about the repertoire and performance.

Three Approaches toward Programming

Three different ways of selecting repertoire for concert performance are listed below. As mentioned before, there are great ideas to be found in books and articles—and more appear with the publication of each new journal issue. These three are basic selection frameworks that can be modified to meet the needs of your particular situation.

The Core Approach

- The choral teacher selects a "core repertory" of pieces that is to be learned by each student during the three years of enrollment. Different pieces are learned by the sixth grade chorus, the seventh grade chorus, and the eighth grade chorus. When they complete grade 8, students will have sung the same core repertoire as students who graduate before or after them. Choral teachers choose repertoire to supplement the core throughout the year, but this supplemental repertoire changes from year to year.
- This approach works best for teachers with limited budgets (the core stays the same) and for teachers who want to ensure that students learn the same basic concepts throughout their choral experience.
- For teachers who see their choirs in groupings that cross grade levels (there are sixth, seventh, and/or eighth graders in the same choirs) a variation is to choose three sets of core repertoire; one set is performed in "Year A," another in "Year B," and another in "Year C."

The Checklist Approach

- The choral teacher fills a checklist for a predetermined concert program; each repertoire selection represents a specific genre or style.
- An example of a six-selection concert programming checklist might be:

1. Opener: fast, repeated rhythmic and melodic motifs; begins in unison; piano accompaniment
2. Challenge: the most musically difficult piece of the program; perhaps in a foreign language
3. Transition: a choral "art song" or folksong; long legato lines; meaningful text; perhaps with instrumental obbligato
4. World Music (not North American): rhythmic piece performed with stylistic/cultural authenticity; perhaps including limited movement; with appropriate instrumental accompaniment
5. North American: piece representing a culture or musical style within North America; perhaps a spiritual, jazz, folksong, or nontraditional choral setting (Native American chants, pieces involving vocal improvisation, and so forth)
6. Patriotic: a nationalistic piece employing more than the commonly known verses; perhaps using larger instrumental forces than in previous pieces in the concert (such as brass or percussion); perhaps allowing for audience members to join in singing the final verse

- This approach works well for teachers who have limited time to search for new music; music can be easily categorized as teachers attend workshops, conferences, or receive new repertoire from publishers.

The Theme Approach

- The choral teacher keeps lists (or octavos) grouped by specific themes found in the text or musical qualities chosen by the composer; concert repertoire is then determined from this limited number of selections.
- Examples of themes:
  o Water (rain, liquid, snow, ice, fog)
  o Love (pursuit, enchantment, spurned, unrequited)
  o Lullabies (from different musical cultures)
  o Transportation (trains, autos, planes, boats)

    o Continents (one piece representing each continent)

    o American Female Poets

    o Geography (mountains, rivers, oceans, plains, trails)

    o Seasons

- This approach works especially well in schools that have large interdisciplinary projects or themes that are planned well in advance.

Chapter Six

Recruiting Singers

The adults who will sing in a church or community choir tomorrow are walking through the hallways of your school today. Unless these students begin to make music during the elementary or intermediate years, they may become burned-out, overstressed adults who lack a creative element in their lives.

Recruiting students for school performance ensembles can present a challenge. Most middle school students are presented with a massive array of choices for use of their extracurricular time. If your choral program functions largely beyond the school day, be prepared to deal with scheduling conflicts with other activities, such as team sports, clubs, private music and dance lessons, karate, church activities, and family responsibilities.

In some cases, you may be able to negotiate some leeway with other teachers. For example, to eliminate one of the biggest conflicts for students, try negotiating an attendance policy with the school's athletic department staff. This policy can be stated succinctly, for example, "Students involved in the athletic program are allowed one excused absence per week for the purpose of rehearsing in a school-sponsored musical ensemble such as band or choir."

Recruiting strategies aren't too difficult to employ if you methodically choose a few that seem suitable to your school and your own temperament. Allow plenty of time for publicity efforts to work for you before you abandon one recruiting strategy for another one. There are four categories of recruiters with whom you can work: your current students, other teachers, parents, and external groups.

CURRENT STUDENTS

The best recruiters are enthusiastic students who are already members of the choir. Here's what they can do on their own or with a little help from you:

- Create a "buddy system" matching each current choral student with a friend or acquaintance who is a potential chorister.
- Have students recommend potential singers.
- Have students give recruitment speeches or announcements.
- Send interested students an invitation to your next concert, complete with reserved seating.
- Have candidates for the choral group stand to be recognized during the concert.
- Schedule a mini-concert at elementary schools in the district presented by one of your choirs. Feature boys and girls separately.
- Select your literature carefully for elementary recruitment concerts. Perform at least one difficult number and introduce it with care. Lighter numbers should show a high level of artistry.
- Have your current choir members wear their sports uniforms to the recruitment concerts. Also recognize those choir members in honor societies, clubs, and so forth. This will encourage the "I want to be just like him or her!" responses from the younger students.
- Distribute a flyer or information sheet with a memorable slogan such as "Choir: It's Tonally Awesome." On the back of the flyer, print a list of the students currently in your choirs. Have the students at assemblies circle each name they recognize.
- For every performance, include a piece that is either well-known by the audience or easily taught. Encourage the audience to sing along with your choir when that piece is performed.
- Plan ahead to incorporate elementary choir students into the middle school choir for the performance of a special song by the joined choirs.
- If you cannot visit the elementary schools, try having your current students make a ten- or fifteen-minute "choir commercial" video and send it to the music teacher instead.

OTHER TEACHERS

Working with fellow professionals in different fields can be mutually beneficial. Here are a few ideas:

- Find out which faculty members sang in their all-state choirs, high school musicals, college choirs, or some similar choral group, and establish a faculty choir. Male faculty members may be able to encourage the potential boy singers sitting in the audience. Having the faculty perform once or twice a year, for example, with eighth graders, may enable you to perform more challenging music you may not be able to do otherwise. Make certain that the faculty ensemble presents material that attracts students' attention. If the faculty choir is interested in doing only pop music and its performances aren't top-notch, then you can just imagine how the students will roll their eyes when they hear the adult group. Keep your objective in mind—getting nonsinging students interested in choir—by seeing things from the students' perspective.
- Ask elementary teachers to recommend students to your choirs. Follow this recommendation with a meeting or friendly "Voice Placement Hearing" (see chapter 2) and a congratulatory letter from the principal or supervisor.
- Have your choir give your principal an "Arts Administrator" award if there has been any effort to help your program. Goodwill goes a long way in promoting choir membership.
- Work with other faculty members to schedule interdisciplinary units with Civil War songs, South African protest songs, or other songs appropriate to units they may be teaching. Foreign language teachers are also excellent resources for developing interdisciplinary units.

PARENTS

If parents are kept informed, they may be motivated to encourage their children to join choir. Here are a couple of ideas that will show what belonging to middle school choir can do for its members.

- Write a letter to the parents of incoming students, including a list of all the academic honors, musical achievements, clubs, and athletic teams represented by your current choir members.
- Write a congratulatory letter to the parents of any child recommended to your choir by an elementary teacher.

EXTERNAL RECRUITERS

Positive outside influences can also encourage a child to join choir. Some ideas:

- In addition to classic choral works, feature recordings of various doo wop, jazz, and a cappella groups in your general music classes to showcase the ranges of male and female singing voices.
- Invite successful alumni to perform with the choir.
- Bring in area college voice majors as models who can assist your students in establishing their own realistic goals for singing.
- If at all possible, begin an adult community choir. A group like this influences both parents and school boards—especially if you can get a school board member to join. If a community choir already exists in your area, join it or offer your talents as an accompanist or rehearsal assistant.
- Try enlisting BHS, the Barbershop Harmony Society, and their affiliated organization for female voices, the Sweet Adelines. If four, eight, or twelve of your students can maintain individual vocal lines, barbershop music can be an invaluable tool for teaching music reading, vocal independence, vowel formation, balance, and blend. The four parts of the male barbershop quartet (bass, baritone, lead, and tenor) correspond well to the stages of the changing male voice, making barbershop singing particularly applicable for middle school boys.
- Many materials are available for the developing barbershop ensemble, including the Young Men in Harmony Songbook with an extremely helpful section for choral music teachers new to barbershop; videos of students in barbershop ensembles; and music for three- and four-part male ensembles. The Young Women in Harmony Student Songbook

provides a collection of songs voiced for young women's four-part barbershop harmony.

- Invite area adult choral ensembles to perform at your school concerts.

BUT, IT'S ALL ABOUT THE MUSIC!

In all your recruiting efforts, remember that students will be most eager to join a program that appears vibrant, energetic, and growing. Use a combination of the ideas in this chapter, coupled with your personal knowledge of your school and town, to allow students to see the broad musical community that is available to them. The best advertising will be your choirs performing successfully and your students growing musically. Success yields success, and everyone wants to be part of a successful endeavor. Be positive, upbeat, and unflaggingly enthusiastic about music, singing, and your students.

Chapter Seven

The Young Adolescent

Middle school teachers recognize that even though early adolescence is a distinctive developmental stage of life, the general public has limited understanding of these ten to fifteen year olds. The National Middle School Association (www.nmsa.org) has developed broad sets of research-based guidelines to assist teachers in developing instructional methods to meet the needs of these young adolescents. The contents of this chapter build upon those guidelines to provide background information about these youngsters and specific implications for choral music teachers.

The accelerated physical and personal development that occurs during this period is the greatest in the human life cycle and is marked by great variance in both the timing and rate of growth. These are the years during which each individual forms his or her adult personality, basic values, and attitudes—those things that determine one's behavior. For a variety of reasons, young adolescents today reach physical maturity at an earlier age than their grandparents and they acquire apparent sophistication earlier than in previous generations.

SOME GENERAL CHARACTERISTICS
OF YOUNG ADOLESCENTS

- They seek autonomy and independence.
- They are by nature explorers, curious and adventuresome.
- They have intellectual capacities seldom tapped by traditional schooling.

- They learn best through interaction and activity rather than by listening.
- They seek interaction with adults and opportunities to engage in activities that have inherent value.
- Their physical and social development emerge as priorities at the same time as they become sensitive, vulnerable, and emotional.
- They are open to influence by the significant others in their lives. Will you be one of those significant others?

PHYSICAL GROWTH

Young adolescents experience rapid, irregular physical growth and the bodily changes they undergo may cause awkward, uncoordinated movements. They vary greatly in their rate of physical maturation, with girls maturing approximately one and one-half to two years earlier than boys. Hormonal changes for both boys and girls may cause them to experience restlessness and fatigue. At the same time, they need daily physical activity because of increasing overall levels of energy. Both boys and girls are concerned with bodily changes that accompany sexual maturation. This provides opportunities for choral music teachers to emphasize the physical changes that cause the adolescent voice change in both boys and girls.

EMOTIONAL AND PSYCHOLOGICAL DEVELOPMENT

Young adolescents experience mood swings with peaks of intensity and unpredictability. They may feel a need to release energy, resulting in sudden, apparently meaningless outbursts of activity. They seem to become increasingly independent, searching for adult identity and acceptance. Part of this process is an increasing concern about peer acceptance. Related to this is an increase in self-consciousness, with low self-esteem in both boys and girls. Young adolescents in general are highly sensitive to personal criticism.

During the middle school years, students increasingly behave in ways associated with their gender. This might open the door for single-gender rehearsals or choirs. The texts that these choirs sing should be substantive and related to current issues because adolescents become concerned about major societal issues. Even though they begin to focus on the world around them, young adolescents tend to believe that personal problems, feelings, and experiences are unique to themselves. Middle school students are psychologically vulnerable, if only because at no other stage in development are they so likely to encounter so many differences between themselves and others.

INTELLECTUAL DEVELOPMENT

Young adolescents display a wide range of individual intellectual development as they transition from concrete thinking to abstract thinking. They are intensely curious and have a wide range of intellectual pursuits, few of which are sustained. Many students will dabble at choral music, only to withdraw—and sometimes join again. This is a normal part of adolescence, and choral music teachers need to carefully consider how they respond to students who announce they're quitting choir. Will we leave the door open for them to rejoin a choir, whether that happens next week, next month, next year, or five years from now?

Middle school students prefer active over passive learning activities and enjoy peer interaction during learning activities. They have a need for approval and may be easily discouraged by teacher feedback that focuses on the student ("You did a great job") rather than on the results of their efforts ("You did a great job figuring out the rhythm to 'Niska Banja'").

SOCIAL DEVELOPMENT

Young adolescents feel a need to belong to a group, with peer approval becoming more important as adult approval decreases in importance. For that reason, group work can become an increasingly important instructional strategy during choral music rehearsals. But it is important to remember that teachers need to teach the social skills necessary for this group work to be successful. In general, and especially in boys, the development of social skills lags behind intellectual and physical maturity. This is part of brain development and needs to be considered when planning rehearsals. It is not appropriate to scold students for immature social behavior that is beyond their control.

Middle school students look for other, more mature individuals that they can use as role models. They often adopt the slang and behavioral characteristics they assume will make them "part of the group," only to find those attempts misfire in actual social situations. This is all part of trying to gain acceptance with their peers—and occasionally with you. It is most difficult for students who are slower to mature. Young adolescents find themselves in the unenviable position of having to adjust to the social adeptness of early maturing girls and the athletic successes of early maturing boys, especially if they themselves are maturing at a slower rate.

MORAL DEVELOPMENT

Young adolescents are idealistic, and they desire to make the world a better place and become socially useful. Their cognitive development allows a gradual transition from self-centeredness to considering the rights and feelings of others. As a result, middle school students often show compassion for those who are suffering and have concerns for animals and environmental issues.

Through the process of adolescent development, middle school students move from accepting the moral judgments of adults toward the development of their own values (even though they may eventually adopt the moral positions of influential adults). However, young adolescents are often quick to see flaws in others but slow to see their own faults. That is one reason that feedback from teachers needs to be specific to the tasks they ask students to perform rather than generalized praise ("great job!").

IN THE CHORAL REHEARSAL

Middle school students present numerous contradictions to their choral music teachers. At this time of great physical and vocal change, these youngsters are often sad about the vocal change, missing the childhood voices they once had. These students are fiercely independent yet they long for their teachers to provide structure and guidance. They'll state that they dislike the choral repertoire you choose, but they'll clamor to sing it repeatedly once it's been learned.

Rather than dismiss these contradictions, choral teachers must recognize and embrace them. The physical, emotional, and intellectual changes of young adolescence lead to greater levels of musicianship, vocal skill, and artistic knowledge. We need to provide achievable challenges for these young singers. If we don't, boredom may result in the students choosing more interesting and achievable activities instead of choral music. We can respond by selecting repertoire, designing rehearsals, and planning performances to meet the needs of these young adolescent musicians.

Middle school students report that they experience music learning most powerfully when they are engaged with other students in activities that develop and challenge their skills, when they are invited to make music both individually and collectively with their peers, when they have opportunities to interact personally with their teachers, and when they experience several changes in grouping and activity within rehearsals.

ADAPT, BUILD, AND CHALLENGE

In summary, middle school choral music teachers must do three things:

A = Adapt rehearsals to the changing needs of young adolescents.
B = Build on what students know and build toward what they need to know.
C = Challenge students in ways that match their skill levels.

The ideas provided throughout this book are designed to address these three ABCs of choral music education for young adolescents.

Chapter Eight

The Young Adolescent Voice

Imagine your seventh grade choral ensemble in rehearsal. In a pianissimo moment, Brad's voice cracks with a force audible to all. How do he and his classmates react to this event? It depends on the environment you have created and the knowledge you have encouraged your students to acquire. Such potentially embarrassing moments can be defused if you have taken care to explain the changing voice and invited the students to tell you about their vocal changes.

We know that all of our vocal sounds mark our progress along a continuum of vocal development that begins before birth and lasts throughout life. The adolescent voice change is only one stage of that development. If students understand some basic concepts of vocal physiology, they will have invaluable information that can help them musically through the early teenage years and for many years of music making to come.

The adolescent vocal change is prompted by hormonal changes in the body that may begin as early as grade 4 and are associated with puberty. During puberty, the male vocal folds increase in both length and thickness. The average increase in length of about ten millimeters lowers the range an octave or more. Of concern to the music educator is that the lengthening occurs at different rates in different boys.

The male adolescent voice isn't the only one that changes—so does the female voice, but it changes more in quality than in range. Because male adolescent singers will experience changes in both range and the sensation of vocal coordination, choral music teachers need to take these issues into account when selecting repertoire and rehearsal methods. This chapter is an introduction to current knowledge about male and female adolescent voices. You are encouraged to seek more detailed supplementary information during the earliest professional development opportunities of your career.

THE DEVELOPING MALE VOICE

The issue of the changing adolescent voice, and the boy's developing voice in particular, has confronted music educators since the dawn of the profession. The seemingly unpredictable adolescent voice has been so perplexing to musicians that many educators have developed theories of changing voice. Attempts have been made to define ways of nurturing and classifying the changing voice so that teachers can develop choral ensembles that meet the students' vocal, emotional, and aesthetic needs.

When the musculature that operates the vocal folds changes position rapidly, boys' voices are sometimes said to "crack," although this term is not at all accurate. Basically, the boy has just experienced a sudden shift in the musculature instead of the smoothly controlled muscular coordination he was expecting. These sudden adjustments are related to the developing musculature around the larynx and are part of normal vocal maturation. Boys who develop the skills of mixing the head and chest registers prior to the voice change are often more successful in mixing the registers that occur during and after the change.

Actually, it may be advantageous to refer to the ways singers experience muscle usage rather than describing registers. After all, under optimal conditions, singers control their muscle use, while registers can seem to be comparatively unchangeable. Try using the terms "heavy mechanism" (chest voice) and "light mechanism" (head voice). Voice scientists, voice teachers, and singing coaches increasingly prefer these more descriptive terms.

If we want every child to sing throughout adolescence, we need to understand the stages and qualities of voice that young people are likely to experience at this time. John Cooksey identified several of the similarities agreed upon by prominent theorists studying the changing male voice:

- The voice change occurs concurrently with other pubertal developments.
- Most published choral literature is inadequate for groups of males with changing voices.

- Irregular patterns of voice change may cause unpredictability, particularly if boys are forced into inappropriate vocal ranges.
- In the middle and junior high years (through grades 9 or 10), many different stages of vocal development exist in any group of young men.
- Different voices mature at different rates.
- Individual and group voice testing is necessary.
- Students need to be informed about the changing voice.
- Continued development of good vocal technique is essential throughout the process of vocal change.

In the mid-1970s, Cooksey began to collect and conduct research in an effort to determine what actually happens physiologically and acoustically to the boy's voice throughout the change process. He identified six voice change stages that have been substantiated by numerous research studies involving thousands of young men worldwide. Each boy progresses through the stages at different rates, pausing in some stages and rapidly passing through others. Some young men experience smooth transitions between stages, while others encounter more abrupt progressions. A boy moves sequentially through each stage before eventually settling into his mature voice during the late teen years.

The six stages of male voice change are illustrated in the accompanying chart. Note that Cooksey identified a range and tessitura for each stage. These general guidelines are not meant to imply that each boy's individual voice matches each stage identically, and the ranges represent the boy's normal singing voice, not the falsetto. Although young men find the light mechanism ("head voice") or falsetto more difficult to access during some stages, Cooksey advocates having them sing throughout their entire ranges to encourage healthy development of the vocal mechanism.

As young men progress through the stages of vocal development, the lower limit of the range descends rapidly and then stabilizes; the upper limit follows the descent more gradually. This effect is analogous to a toy slinky descending a staircase. This could be why the voice may seem to change overnight, although these apparently sudden extensions of the lower range are simply a continuation of the change process.

Cooksey's terminology was developed to indicate that these voice types are unique and unlike the standard classifications of "tenor" and "bass."

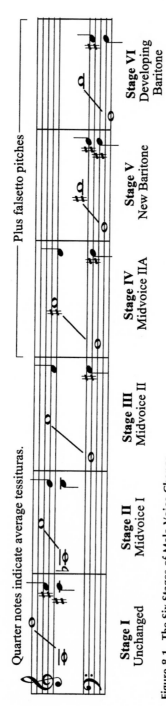

Figure 8.1. The Six Stages of Male Voice Change

Source: Adapted from Cooksey, J. (2000). Voice transformation in male adolescents. In L. Thurman & G. Welch (Eds.), *Bodymind and voice: Foundations of voice education* (p. 726). Iowa City: The National Center for Voice and Speech.

Notes: 1. Approximate ranges and tessituras during male vocal change.
2. Falsetto begins to emerge at the Midvoice IIA stage.

A fourteen-year-old baritone certainly doesn't sound like a twenty-four-year-old baritone. Likewise, many composers of children's choir music now write for "treble voices" instead of sopranos and altos.

What Do We Know about the Male Changing Voice? (A Very Brief Summary)

- Boys experience the adolescent voice change in a sequence of stages that occur at varying rates. The result is a predictable progression marked by periods of growth and stabilization.
- Recent scientific research confirms that all normally healthy boys progress through the same sequence of stages, with some rebounding to higher pitch levels after the final stage. (Ask an adult tenor if he ever had bass notes—most did!)
- The hormonal secretions that activate puberty also initiate the process of vocal change. This begins at different times in different boys, as early as ages nine or ten and as late as age fourteen.
- The first vocal sign is that the upper pitch range becomes unstable and more effortful with a vocal quality that becomes slightly breathy. For most boys, the peak of the voice change (when falsetto begins to emerge) occurs somewhere in the twelfth or thirteenth year. The voice change continues through the college years. One can expect many stages of voice change in groups of seventh grade boys.
- The best way to assess a boy's voice is to identify the entire vocal range, excluding falsetto. When we only notice the lowest pitches, it may seem as though the change process occurs very quickly. But the boys' newly acquired low pitches are only part of the change process. Other important factors are tessitura, voice quality, register development, and the average fundamental speaking pitch.
- Sometimes boys try to sing an octave lower then they're supposed to because they're imitating a female teacher who is singing at the very bottom of her range—with the best of intentions, of course. The reverse often occurs when adult men sing in their falsetto when modeling for treble singers—and the trebles sing an octave higher than expected.
- The cracking in adolescent boys' voices is largely a result of laryngeal muscles growing at different rates, coupled with some thickening of the vocal folds. This effect can be somewhat minimized by encouraging

boys to sing prior to and throughout the voice change, helping boys adjust to the new vocal techniques required by their developing vocal musculature, and encouraging them to sing with their new voice as well as their falsetto when it becomes available to them.

- Adolescent male voices should not be expected to sound like adult voices. Teachers may consider using labels other than "tenor" and "baritone" to identify parts in printed octavos (many publishers already do this).

It is the teacher's responsibility to be aware of the latest scientific information and the musical literature available for boys during this period of development. Once you become aware of the current and future vocal capabilities of all of your students, you will be able to share that information with them and engage in music making that is healthy and developmentally appropriate.

THE DEVELOPING FEMALE VOICE

The information presented in this section is based on the work of Lynne Gackle. Dr. Gackle's research continues to influence our profession's knowledge of the maturing adolescent female voice. One of the most concise yet highly informative sources for information about changing voices (male and female) is Dr. Gackle's chapter, "Changing Voice," in *Music at the Middle Level: Building Strong Programs* (MENC, 1994). Gackle, who studies the changing female voice, has identified four stages that occur during a girl's adolescence. These are shown in the accompanying figure.

The female voice change has not been studied as extensively as the male voice change, but Gackle's ongoing research notes that changes in the female voice do occur but are different than those that occur in males. The onset of female adolescent voice change occurs with the beginning of menstruation, a physical development that is occurring earlier and earlier with each passing decade.

As you can see in the chart describing the four stages of female voice change, the overall range actually expands slightly to encompass slightly higher and lower pitches. But the most noticeable change is that the timbre of the voice darkens as it matures, progressing from a tone color possibly described as "light blue" to a tone color somewhat more like "darker

Quarter notes indicate average tessituras.

Stage I
Prepubertal

Stage II
Premenarcheal

Stage IIB
Postmenarcheal

Stage III
Young Adult

Figure 8.2. The Four Stages of Female Voice Change
Source: Adapted from Gackle, L. (1994). Changing voice. In J. Hinckley (Ed.), *Music at the middle level: Building strong programs* (p. 56). Reston, VA: MENC.

Notes: 1. Approximate ranges and tessituras during female vocal change.
2. Complete development of the adult voice continues after Stage III.

blue." This change is largely attributable to a thickening, rather than a lengthening, of the vocal folds. This vocal fold thickening, and the other physical changes in adolescent girls, occurs in stages over several years. The thickening does not occur all at once, however, and the two vocal folds will thicken at slightly different rates. When that occurs, the vocal folds will not close completely to allow clear phonation. The result will be a breathy tone. This is completely normal and care should be taken that girls don't exert excessive muscular force to try and eliminate the breathy sound. The breathiness will diminish naturally as maturation proceeds.

Some Key Points about the Female Developing Voice

- There are no sopranos or altos during adolescence. Girls' voices are basically light sopranos. Girls who say they "can't sing that high" are basically responding to changes in muscular sensation. The higher pitches effortlessly sung during childhood now require muscular coordination. Since this is a new sensation, some girls may avoid it, thinking that they are doing something wrong. Gradually work with all girls to sing all available pitches comfortably and confidently. This is best done through the voice coaching you'll provide during the warm-up portions of your rehearsals. Take a long term view of this process, and very gradually bring these girls to trust you, the music, and their newly discovered vocal capabilities.
- Never interpret a strong lower register as a sign that an adolescent girl is (or will become) an alto.
- To work with, rather than against, the developing musculature, look for opportunities for unison singing that focus attention on line, phrasing, and dynamic control.
- Arrange for girls to sing repertoire where the vocal lines have the same range and tessitura so that no girl sings in an inappropriate tessitura for any length of time.
- When singing traditional SA or SSAA repertoire, have singers switch parts so that all girls sing through their entire range and have the opportunity to read various vocal lines.
- Do look for choral repertoire with wide vocal ranges, but don't select repertoire where the tessituras are consistently at the extremes of the lower or upper range.

- As with all else in middle school, always seek to honor the maturity and intellect of girls. Choose texts that are meaningful and substantive. Invite girls to notice their developing voices with the same curiosity as the boys will direct at their own voices.

TALKING TO YOUNG ADOLESCENTS
ABOUT THEIR CHANGING VOICES

The changes in young adolescent voices are to be celebrated. The characteristic sound of adolescent choirs is unique, and it is a sound highly prized by successful middle school choral teachers. Teachers will want to talk to their students about their changing voices so that the students can appreciate the changes that are occurring and will continue to occur throughout adolescence. The following are some general guidelines and some specific strategies for discussing the changing voice in your choral classroom.

Singing Is Not a Gift, but a Skill

Singing is like driving a car. No one can drive a standard transmission car without practice. Over a period of time, the driver develops skills that result in smooth transitions between gears, which results in successful trips. The process of vocal change is analogous to a car trip during which the larynx is learning how to "shift gears" smoothly. To clarify this idea for your students, you may wish to use alternate terms for changing voice such as "developing voice," "expanding voice," or "transforming voice."

We Are Preparing Singers for a Lifetime of Music Making

If adolescent boys can't understand their changing voices, they will likely join that huge, mostly male population of adults embarrassed about their singing abilities. The voice is unlike any other musical instrument because the sound it produces is completely related to the individual producing the sound—we don't have external reeds, finger pads, or valves. Therefore, criticism of the voice may be misinterpreted as a criticism of the person. While maintaining our standards and expectations, we should take every precaution to avoid "emotional ouches" when dealing with these students.

The Developing Voice Bulletin Board

You may wish to develop a chart on which students track their progress through the stages of vocal development. Such a chart also makes a great bulletin board that can remain in the same location for the entire year—a definite bonus for the busy teacher. Begin by taking an entire bulletin board and drawing a grand staff. Divide the staff into measures corresponding to the number of vocal stages you list. You could create up to ten measures, including Gackle's stages I, II, IIB, and III for the girls and the six Cooksey stages for the boys. Use brightly colored markers to draw the range for each voice part in the measure. Have students cut out quarter notes from colored 3 x 5 index cards and write their names on the notes. Determine which voice part is most accurate for each singer by holding voice placement hearings, either in groups or individually. Using thumbtacks, have each student attach his or her quarter note to the bulletin board in the appropriate measure. As each student progresses through the year, have the student move his or her quarter note to the next category when appropriate. Changes in girls' voices will be more subtle than changes in boys' voices. Remind the students that this is not a contest, but a way to track expected vocal changes.

Utilize Familiar Terminology

Introduce the concept of the voice change in familiar, nonthreatening terms. Begin the discussion with a video excerpt of a currently popular male vocal group that uses reasonably healthy vocal technique. It will be left to your discretion to choose groups that span multiple genres from classical to barbershop to pop and jazz. You might continue your discussion by comparing the singers to parts of an engine that function together toward a common goal. This may advance the "transmission" motif discussed earlier. The basic question following the presentation might be, "If all young men begin as trebles, why are there so many different voice types in older men?" As student answers lead to a discussion of the changing voice, you might want to guess the vocal classification of various male faculty members, using whatever terminology is familiar to the students.

Work from Simple to Complex, Known to Unknown

Work from simple to complex when discussing the physiology of the larynx. Use an image such as a balloon. Many teachers use balloons as a physical way to show inhalation and exhalation in the diaphragm area. By stretching and releasing the lip of the balloon, one can vary the pitch of the sound made by the escaping air. Although the actual workings of the voice are somewhat different, this can be a good introduction to the concept of vocal folds that change length to create different pitches. This presentation might be followed by a class discussion with the science teacher about Bernoulli's Law—the scientific principle that explains how the air that passes between the vocal folds draws them together rather than pushes them apart. Such an interdisciplinary approach with the science department could continue with collaborative teaching about vocal anatomy using models and charts.

Show the Larynx in Action

Use a multimedia approach to showing the inner workings of the vocal tract. Investigate the possibility of asking an otolaryngologist to videotape your own or your students' vocal folds using a laryngoscope. (Get parental permission for the students to undergo the procedure.) Medical college and university instructors can perform this procedure and may be willing to work with your school on a joint project. Although students most readily absorb the information if someone they know is taped, Pacific Isle Publishing produces "The Singers' Voice: Vocal Folds," a DVD that includes a laryngeal video of a professional soprano. This DVD alternates real footage with animated, narrated footage. You might consider turning down the volume and providing your own narration using kid-friendly terminology. A teacher's guide is sold separately and includes posters and other pedagogical support materials. Because the real footage may be a bit jarring for young people, seek administrative approval and/or parental permission before showing to your choir.

Vocal Anatomy Resources

The following four resources are recommended for anatomical models of the larynx and vocal tract, pedagogical videos, and other resources about the physical aspects of singing.

Carolina Biological Supply (800-334-5551)
2700 York Road
Burlington, NC 27215
www.carolina.com

The Evolution Store (800-952-3195)
120 Spring Street
New York, NY 10012
www.evolutionnyc.com

Kilgore International, Inc. (800-892-9999)
36 West Pearl Street
Coldwater, MI 49036
www.kilgoreinternational.com

Pacific Isle Publishing (800-284-7043)
4227 S. Bayside Lane
Greenbank, WA 98230
www.excellenceinsinging.com

Encourage Critical Thinking and Problem Solving Skills

When the students seem to be comfortable and curious, pose several questions and let them arrive at their own solutions. Here are several questions for class discussion:

- How might the developing voices in our choir affect our choice of repertoire?
- How is the voice change related to other aspects of adolescence?
- What are our choir's comfortable singing ranges?
- Is there a common range among our male students?

After this discussion, take a piece from your repertoire and work with the students to arrange suitable parts for changing voices. This may take a while, since it draws on so many different aspects of musical knowledge, but you'll be surprised at how many students love this challenge. Another way of having the students arrange for changing voices is to use the existing parts as the basis for a new part. This technique was termed "voice pivoting" by Sally Herman in her 1988 book, *Building a Pyramid of Musicianship* (a highly recommended text for middle school choral teachers).

Prepare for Success

Make sure the foundation exists for musical success at all times. Changing voices are affected by many easily overlooked musical issues. For example, boys, usually tenors, who have been reading pitches from the treble staff for years are suddenly presented with the conundrum of singing those pitches an octave lower than they are printed. Baritones may have to learn to sing in a completely new clef—the bass clef. Also, the standard warm-ups at the beginning of the rehearsal may need to be adapted for changing pitch levels. Try some nonspecific pitch exercises that are updated from early elementary years, such as the tried-and-true "fire siren" and voice exploration techniques.

Provide Quality Vocal Models

Generally, it is more helpful for students to respond to adolescent vocal models rather than to adult vocal models. Encourage some students from the upper grades to demonstrate their singing for your current students. These veterans may also like to share success stories or challenging experiences from their changing voice years. It may be useful to build a library of audio or video recordings of exemplary students for future use.

Sometimes younger males try to manipulate their voices to sound like adult males, including their male voice teachers. Explain to them that this is not necessary and that their voices will mature as they continue to sing.

Female music educators should not use the very bottom of their ranges when singing with adolescent males. This practice sends mixed messages regarding the masculinity of male students' voices and the effort needed to produce those tones. In addition, if a female teacher sings with basses and tenors at their actual pitches, she can do great harm to her own voice. Furthermore, the new basses and tenors may often try to sing an octave lower still, because they'll earnestly strive to match the teacher's vocal production rather than the actual pitch.

Separate Boys and Girls

Work with the changing voices of both girls and boys separately when possible. For instance, an all-male workshop encourages the boys to be more open and honest regarding their voices. Having each boy match a predetermined pitch as part of the lesson is counterproductive. Since each voice is different, work with each boy at the most comfortable pitch in his current range. In this way, you will lead toward rather than begin with pitch matching. Allow students to describe their physical and aural sensations in their own words. You can use their responses to help them build a descriptive vocabulary that is meaningful and comfortable to them.

CHOOSING CHORAL REPERTOIRE
FOR DEVELOPING VOICES

The most important piece of information you can have when choosing repertoire is the vocal capabilities of your students. For example, you will notice that the unison singing range for an average middle school choir encompasses only the interval of a sixth—roughly from G to E in octaves. You may notice that female singers often have a vocal tone quality characterized by breathiness as the vocal folds mature. Upon hearing the individual voices in your choir, you may determine that melodies containing stepwise motion are more appropriate for your singers than repertoire containing numerous skips.

Beginning teachers can only make informed guesses when ordering music for the first time. Once you have worked with your students for even a brief period, you will find that your knowledge of your singers' vocal ranges and the individuality of each voice will help guide you toward challenging and satisfying repertoire choices for the immediate future. Your awareness of the developing adolescent voice will help you to predict the vocal needs of your students further into the year. An annotated list of repertoire that can be easily adapted to any middle school choir can be found in *TIPS: The First Weeks of Middle School Chorus*, published as a companion to the book you are reading.

It is well beyond the scope of this book to cover the fundamentals of singing and voice education. For more detailed material describing vocal technique and the teaching of singing, consult texts such as *Teaching Kids to Sing* by Kenneth H. Phillips and *Choral Pedagogy* (second edition) by Brenda Smith and Robert Thayer Sataloff. For a comprehensive and practical guide to vocal development, anatomy, health, and voice education, see *Bodymind and Voice*, published jointly by the VoiceCare Network and the National Center for Voice and Speech. Keep a vigilant eye for new materials from textbook publishers, from MENC and ACDA journals, and from choral music teachers you respect. These resources will guide you toward a greater understanding of the vocal techniques and musical styles that middle school singers are capable of achieving.

Chapter Nine

Rehearsal Planning

"That conductor knows what she wants and knows how to make it happen." A comment like this can describe a successful choral teacher's rehearsal techniques. When analyzing the interplay between a dynamic conductor and a responsive choir, it is easy to believe that such efficient music making is merely a by-product of that teacher's personality. Satisfying musical experiences are most often the result of planning every detail of rehearsal time based on specific academic and musical goals. A successful teacher prepares each rehearsal carefully, allows for flexibility yet follows the plan, and evaluates the results when the rehearsal is over. The idea is to use the most effective and productive strategies possible during each rehearsal to bring you and your choir closer to your objectives.

As a middle school choral teacher, you want to ensure that your students have the opportunity to learn how to sing freely and confidently. This usually requires observing students individually, whether they are singing alone or in a small group. When band students talk about their instruments, they refer to a physical object they manipulate to create sound. Choral students can talk only about their voices. One of the focal points of middle school rehearsals is helping students to recognize their voices as musical instruments. Asking the student questions such as, "What do you notice about the position of your jaw?" or "How did that feel?" does more to focus attention on the vocal instrument than stating, "Your jaw was too far forward," or "That note was flat."

The rehearsal should focus on the physical skills necessary to produce the sound, the intellectual skills required to analyze choral performances, the technical skills needed to make sense of printed music notation, and the expressive skills called for in performing music. You must ensure that any criticism of a student's voice is directed toward the voice as a musical instrument, not toward the individual who is singing.

You also need to be aware that some students have different preferences for how they learn music. For example, some prefer to see the printed page, while others need to hear the phrase before they can sing it. Other students are physically limited as to what they can see and do in the rehearsal and performance, including those individuals who have difficulty with vision, hearing, movement, or various other challenges. These considerations need to be factored into rehearsal planning.

The best approach to rehearsal planning is moving from the general to the specific, or "top-down" planning. This chapter describes top-down planning from a time span of three years through to individual rehearsals taking place during single class periods. It also presents ideas for structuring rehearsals and specific points for dealing with the first rehearsal of a new chorus.

TOP-DOWN PLANNING

To help retain your sanity amid the flurry of activity that accompanies any middle school music program, plan your major rehearsal goals first. General music teachers have a curriculum stipulating the content to be taught and the sequence in which the content is presented. The choral teacher must also develop structured lessons and rehearsals by looking at his or her schedule and plotting goals over time.

The Three-Year Plan

At the middle school level, teachers normally work with students for three years. What students learn in grade 6 prepares them for grade 7. By the end of grade 8, they should have three years of incrementally acquired knowledge. For your sake as well as the students', planning a three-year learning cycle makes more sense than trying to survive from rehearsal to rehearsal or even from semester to semester.

Before you begin, look at the curriculum being taught in the elementary schools, or better yet, talk to an elementary music teacher to find out what skills students acquire that you can expect to build on. Determine the concepts and musical genres you want your students to learn by the time they graduate from middle school; order the material from simple to complex. Then divide it into three-year increments to calculate about how much should be taught during each year of middle school. Referring to documents such as the National Standards for Arts Education and *Strategies for Teaching Elementary and Middle-Level Chorus* (MENC, 1997) can simplify this task considerably, while ensuring that you help your students meet nationally established goals for music education.

A One-Year Plan

Ideally, your one-year plan will be based on a structured, sequential three-year cycle, although it is possible to plan only a year in advance and still deliver quality instruction. A one-year plan is more detailed than a three-year plan in that you fill in specific concepts and repertoire selections. You can organize a one-year plan by semesters or by concerts. Looking at a yearly plan also gives you a good idea of how many rehearsals you have per concert. You can then judge whether or not you have programmed appropriate repertoire at appropriate levels of difficulty. At this point in the planning, your concern should be that your students will have enough time to meet the demands of the repertoire by concert time or year's end. Later, if you find that your goals were overly ambitious, you may need to restructure future rehearsal plans to reflect your revised goals. After all, each participant in your concerts—whether student, audience member, or conductor—wants to experience choral music that confidently showcases the development of specific skills and knowledge.

The Concert or Semester Plan

Depending on how your yearly schedule is organized, you can now fill in detailed goals for each concert or grading period within each semester. Count the number of rehearsals you have for any given concert and evaluate whether the total number of rehearsals you have accommodates the demands of the repertoire. You should arrive at this plan as close to the beginning of the school year as possible, so that, if you vary from it, you can gauge how far you have strayed.

The Weekly Plan

As a beginning teacher, you may be required to turn in copies of lesson plans to the principal or supervisor on a weekly basis. It will be much easier for you to complete your weekly plans if you have already developed the long-range plans described above.

ORGANIZING THE INDIVIDUAL REHEARSAL

There are several ways to organize the forty or so highly prized minutes of your rehearsal. It is hard to determine which styles are suitable for you and your students without actually trying them. Here are some suggestions:

The Three P's Rehearsal

This is based on a basic tenet of lesson planning with Kodály principles in mind. Each lesson should contain three basic elements. (1) Prepare students for something they will learn in a subsequent lesson. The preparation should provide the prior experience you will call upon during the next lesson ("remember when we did . . . ?"). (2) Present new information or content to the students. This may be the longest segment of your rehearsal. (3) Practice something familiar, something presented in the previous lesson. Ideally, students could use this practice component to link a section of the repertoire learned previously with the newly presented material. The basic premise here is that all three components, Prepare, Present, and Practice, are part of every rehearsal.

The Whole-Part-Whole Rehearsal

This is similar to the Three P's Rehearsal, except that you might think of each segment of the rehearsal (each choral selection rehearsed, perhaps) as involving three stages. In the first Whole section, you would present the material to be rehearsed in as complete form as possible. This might include sight-reading through it or listening to a recording. The purpose here is to give students a sense of what they'll be working toward. In the Part section, individual aspects of the material are methodically rehearsed. These might include rhythmic, pitch, ensemble, or vocal production issues. Then, in the final Whole section, have students sing through (or somehow experience) the material in context so that they can gauge the effect of their Part rehearsal on the larger segment of repertoire. This is extremely helpful for students who ask, "Can't we just sing it through? Why do we have to work on the rhythms?" They do get to "sing it through" but they'll also see the results of the detailed work that you've led them through.

The ABA Rehearsal

This rehearsal begins and ends with familiar music. The pace changes during the middle, when new and detailed work is presented at a slower pace. Principals and supervisors tend to approve of this structure because it mirrors teaching models in other content areas.

The Golden Proportion Rehearsal

The rehearsal is designed to have the greatest intensity approximately two-thirds of the way through the allotted time. In a forty-minute period, you might spend the first thirteen minutes (one-third) in warm-up and organizational activities, followed by reviewing familiar musical material. The next, and most important, portion of the rehearsal focuses on new material, culminating in a performance that links the familiar music with the new. The final thirteen minutes are spent by either polishing previously presented repertoire or introducing music to be learned in subsequent sessions.

The Alternating Rehearsal

Frequent changes of pace in the rehearsal are facilitated by alternating the musical tasks according to familiarity, difficulty, genre, or mood. Experiment with building your rehearsals around pieces with different tempos, languages, dynamic levels, or styles. You might be amused at the notion of following a Brahms folk song with an American cowboy song. Such variations in your rehearsal structure will keep students guessing what comes next—and could provide some humorous moments along the way. Middle school singers generally like this rehearsal style the best.

The "Start Off New" Rehearsal

Although most music educators use the first ten to fifteen minutes of rehearsal for review, the first few minutes of class may be the optimum time for new learning. One way to begin this type of rehearsal is to write this question on the blackboard before the students come into the room: "What piece am I playing and what page am I on?" As they enter, play the new materials on the piano while the students look through their repertoire for the specific piece you are playing. After a few moments, stop playing and have the students see if their guesses are correct. Use this moment to segue into teaching the new materials. Whether or not you use such a strategy to focus students' attention, the presentation of new material at the beginning of a rehearsal may capture their curiosity when they are most eager to learn.

BEFORE THE FIRST REHEARSAL

There are several things you can do to establish yourself by the first day of school. Before you even set foot in the classroom, you should do a little of your own rehearsing, including practicing how you will introduce yourself to the students; how you will describe your expectations of the students, along with basic classroom procedures and attendance policies; and how you will present your plan for the year ahead and some of the work necessary to achieve the performance goals. A few days before school starts, visit the classroom and make certain the physical conditions convey the impression you intend. To avoid students' aimlessly milling around the classroom, decide in advance where they are to sit when they come into your room, even if the seating is unassigned.

Plan an achievable musical task for the first rehearsal. Try to steer away from singing something taught by the former teacher, as this may invite too many comparisons. Decide in advance how you will maintain order during class—what your "quiet" signal will be. (One possibility is to sing a sustained, comfortable pitch on an "ooh" vowel, with each student who hears it joining in his or her own octave until the entire choir is singing the same pitch.)

Prepare thoroughly, but be utterly realistic during this first rehearsal—let the students know exactly what you planned for this first class, follow through on it, and tell them what to expect during the next rehearsal. If there are to be choir officers, announce these positions and the anticipated selection procedure. The first meeting of your choir should focus on the goals of the entire group. Let the students know that you plan to do voice testing or placement in the near future and circulate a sign-up sheet so that they can decide when to sing for you. Deferring vocal placement hearings will allow the students to become more familiar with you before singing individually.

ACHIEVING SUCCESS IN EACH REHEARSAL

Before you begin a rehearsal, ask yourself if you can sustain the energy needed to achieve the goals you've planned. If not, moderate the goals or redesign the rehearsal to meet the effort you can bring to it.

A few concepts apply to every rehearsal that determine its overall quality. Singing through a piece and seeing what happens can occasionally be presented as a challenge, but it should not be the standard pattern students use to learn new pieces. Building upon the students' prior knowledge and taking the time to develop a logical, sequential presentation of new musical concepts can expedite students' learning and lessen the wear and tear on you.

Your students need to understand that they're part of the learning process, not passive recipients of information. To that end, spend less time talking about music than you spend having students make music. Try recording a rehearsal and then analyzing your use of the time. Many highly successful conductors regularly record their rehearsals so that they can better direct the efforts of both their students and themselves in subsequent sessions.

Male and female students need to feel equally secure that you are addressing their needs and concerns. Praising students with well-earned comments about their music-making efforts—both individually and as an ensemble—will draw singers in and help them maintain enough focus to meet the goals you've set. Make certain that your praise is specifically oriented toward the student's musical work rather than just saying "nice job" or "good work." Students interpret teacher feedback as more meaningful when it is tied toward something specific that they've done, such as "I noticed that the rhythm work we did in the warm-up really improved the Treble 2 rhythms in 'Niska Banja.' You should be pleased with that improvement!"

Finally, ask yourself if you would have enjoyed being a singer at your own rehearsal. Your answer will please you or spur you on to corrective action!

BUILDING FOR THE FUTURE

When you have determined what each student should know at each grade level, begin teaching toward those goals with your youngest students, usually sixth graders. However, don't automatically assume that the seventh and eighth graders know what you need them to know. During your first year, tread lightly when making demands on the older students. You may find that you have to reteach many concepts the students should have learned in earlier grades. Or you may not be able to do the repertoire you have chosen for your eighth graders because they lack the skills to perform a particular work.

Keep choosing (and re-choosing) repertoire that matches the skills of your students. Yes, there need to be musical challenges, but these should be just slightly beyond what students can do without your help. Any more difficulty will result in student frustration, while too little challenge will result in boredom.

Keep your eye on the prize: the sixth graders should be right on target with their knowledge and skills within two years.

REHEARSAL LESSON PLANS?

Planning a rehearsal is much like riding a bicycle. You know how to ride a bike, from preparing the bicycle for the trip, mounting the bike, balancing, pedaling, braking, and so on. You probably know the route you will take and can preview it using your imagination. But what if there's a detour and you need to take a new, unexpected route? The new route may get you to the destination, but the uphills, downhills, and curves will be a little bit unfamiliar. However, you can rest assured that your skills of shifting smoothly and navigating traffic will get you there.

The same is true for choir rehearsals. No matter how well you study your scores, know the vocal parts, and plan instructional strategies, the students' response may mean you have to take a slightly different route in order to get to your intended choral "destination" for that rehearsal.

For that reason, lesson plans that are listed as "step 1, step 2" and so on will not work in choral rehearsals if they're too specific. Too much depends on how students respond, and "step 3" might not be the right thing to do when the rehearsal is underway.

It's better to simply use a rehearsal plan format that contains three columns: column 1—time (estimated time for each segment of the rehearsal); column 2—segment (warm-up, announcements, sight-reading, repertoire title, and so on); and column 3—activities (the sequence that you intend to follow and the instructional methods you will use during each segment). The activities listed in column 3, then, can be followed exactly as you have written, but they can just as easily be reordered or changed as necessary.

TOP TEN QUESTIONS FOR REHEARSAL PLANNING

No matter how detailed your lesson plans for choral rehearsals with young adolescents, strive to keep the following questions in mind when planning each rehearsal of your choirs.

1. Did you include multiple shifts of activity, focus, and/or location?
2. Did you include rehearsal strategies that facilitate student thinking and conversation, rather than only teacher-oriented strategies?
3. Did you include opportunities for student interaction with peers?
4. Did you include opportunities for students to interact with you individually if necessary?
5. Did you include instructional segments that:

    a. Prepare
    b. Present
    c. Practice?

6. Did you include vocal warm-ups and vocalises specific to the challenges of the repertoire?
7. Did you include vocal exercises interspersed throughout the rehearsal as helpful reminders for the students?

8. Did you include physical gestures or movements specific to the challenges of the repertoire?
9. Did you include activities where all students are involved though your attention is focused on one group?
10. Did you include a group-processing segment (self-assessment) that informs what will happen in the following rehearsal?

RESPONDING TO THE CHOIR

There are two basic duties of the teacher during choral rehearsals: (1) present the repertoire and related skills, and (2) respond to the choir's work. Teachers can determine how they will complete the first task (presenting) as they sketch their overall rehearsal plans. The second task (responding) is more difficult to predetermine and requires a great deal of skill and sensitivity.

Effective response to the choir's work involves the cycle of error *prediction*, error *detection*, and error *correction*. Choral music teachers complete this cycle many times during each minute of the rehearsal. Care and judgment is needed to determine which errors to correct and which to ignore. Some teachers believe that any error is significant; these tend to be ineffective choral music teachers because the choristers perceive them as overly critical and pedantic. Rather, the teacher needs to determine which errors precipitate other errors. Many small errors will disappear as larger issues are resolved. Use the time between rehearsals to decode any persistent errors, decipher the underlying problem, and define the best course of action toward achieving a positive result.

WHEN ALL ELSE FAILS

Take a moment to recall why you chose this profession. Two of the likely reasons are that you love making music with other singers and you have specific musical capabilities that allow you to be successful making music with other singers. Your musicianship is your greatest asset as a choral music teacher. There will be times when lesson plans have to be abandoned, when rehearsals don't proceed as planned, when the students respond differently than you expected, and when the day just throws you a curveball or two. You need to examine your plans and determine how to be more productive when these instances occur in the future. But, in the immediacy of these moments, just *be musical.*

Teaching is not a lesson plan. Choral music is not a rehearsal. Teaching and choral music exist in the interactions between you and your students. Rely on your musicianship. It's what got you here in the first place!

Chapter Ten

Teaching Strategies for Rehearsals

Planning for the individual rehearsals of your choir provides the opportunity to make the most creative choices of your school year. Middle school youngsters often clamor to enroll in choral ensembles because music can be presented in so many ways that appeal to the strengths and affinities of a wide variety of students. Students in choral music rehearsals can be engaged in learning experiences while standing, sitting, or moving; in small groups or in large ensembles; playing teacher-constructed vocal games or quietly listening; and teaching other students or monitoring their own individual progress.

Among the myriad ways in which students can learn in the choral music classroom, you will decide which ways are most appropriate for the music to be presented and the students who are involved. You may certainly develop traditional lesson plans, such as those in which students respond to the visual and verbal instructions of the teacher. This chapter will present many ideas for lesson plan components that may not be traditional, but which you may draw upon for ideas when you are looking for variety or when you have a specific rehearsal situation you need to address. Remember that the choral rehearsal is limited only by your imagination, coupled with your knowledge of the repertoire and your students.

SOME REMINDERS ABOUT
THE ADOLESCENTS WE TEACH

Researchers have confirmed a few things that we intuitively know about working with young adolescents. Here are a few key points that can help us decide on the best teaching strategies to incorporate into our choral rehearsals.

- Students need classroom and rehearsal environments that they view as comfortable, nurturing, and with high levels of teacher support.
- Young adolescents like interesting texts and repertoire that features frequent changes in tempo, texture, rhythm, and so on.
- Students like achievable challenges, not challenges that are too high (stressful) or too low (boring).
- Young adolescents need opportunities for both individual and collective music making, including occasions where they sense that their teachers are making music with them (rather than directing them).
- Middle school students need opportunities to talk and interact with their peers while learning. We can use this to our advantage by providing the topics and structures for these conversations!
- Young people need frequent changes in grouping, location, and activity within the rehearsal (changes should occur about every twelve minutes for an average group of middle school students).
- Adolescent boys need to be located near the teacher (instead of in the back of the room) because of developmental issues regarding hearing and how they interpret visual cues. They need lots of physical activity outlets and dislike lots of "teacher talk." In general, adolescent boys respond well to brief (three or four minute) games and competitions that have clearly defined parameters.
- Adolescent girls need personal attention from the teacher even though they may appear disinterested. They rely much more on verbal and visual cues than on teaching strategies that involve physical activity. Although there are always exceptions, adolescent girls don't appreciate games and competitions in the classroom where there is any risk of being viewed as a failure.

Above all, young adolescents respond to teachers who present high quality musical experiences that are developmentally appropriate and artistically satisfying.

SEQUENCE YOUR TEACHING

No matter which strategies and techniques you choose when developing individual rehearsal activities, it is important to have a plan for how to teach any given concept. One logical way to teach a concept in the rehearsal is to break the process into three steps:

• Present the information or task.
• Encourage student response or interaction with the information or task.
• Provide feedback to the students.

Try not to interrupt the flow of this sequence by focusing your singers on one task, such as breath control of a long phrase, and then giving feedback about something else, with an observation such as, "The third note of the phrase was flat." When your feedback is unrelated to the task you asked your students to undertake, middle school students will quickly become convinced that you are not really paying attention to them and their efforts.

Planning the tasks you give to your choirs in advance truly directs their learning. If you wait until an ensemble is rehearsing to decide on the task, your singers will have determined the content of the lesson instead of you! Successful teachers lead students toward correct responses—including satisfying performances—through a well-planned rehearsal structure that includes appropriate feedback.

GETTING STUDENTS' ATTENTION

Getting any student's attention can be a challenge. The physiological changes during adolescence include sudden shifts in hormone levels within the bodies and brains of your students. These changes in hormone levels can affect a student's ability to maintain attention. You may notice, for example, that one of your middle school students may be fixated on a bug crawling across the floor at one moment, and he is completely focused on your every word in the next moment. Some students have more difficulty than others with maintaining attention. If you take a closer look at what the specific attentional difficulty is, you can then build targeted activities into your rehearsals to meet the needs of individual students. Sometimes activities can follow the lesson plan for the rehearsal. At other times, you may have to abandon the lesson plan and choose a rehearsal strategy to meet the exact situation at hand. Knowing that you have multiple options for teaching any concept can be reassuring.

The following paragraphs group various components of attention into general categories and offer multiple suggestions for helping students manage them. Because of the variety of students, these suggestions are by no means limited to the categories in which they are placed. By experimenting with these ideas individually, you will soon develop a repertoire of techniques to call upon as they seem appropriate.

Helping Students Focus Attention

One of the most difficult challenges for any youngster is to focus attention on what is really important. Asking basic questions such as, "What do you think we should do now?" will intrigue attentive students and arouse the interest of inattentive ones. If you plan to be away from school, have students design the day's rehearsal for the substitute. Or have them plan the next day's lesson with you. When you follow through with it, they'll be paying attention to see if everything planned has been covered and in the right order. Of course, you can always leave something out and see which student picks up on your purposeful omission!

Another way of encouraging students to focus attention is by creating audio recordings of rehearsals and then asking the class to listen and comment on specific components of their performances. Responses to these questions could be written in student "choir journals" that are maintained through the year. Be specific about what you expect from the students and use the opportunity to increase their vocabulary of musical terms so that they can accurately describe what they hear. Have them listen for individual notes or phrases; for example, "Listen for the [a] vowel in the alto part. How could the altos change their tongue position to improve the sound?"

Another option is to choose a few students to be "rehearsal ears," who listen to and comment on a portion of the live rehearsal. Students might include the "ears'" responses in their choir journals. They might also use the journals to summarize the accomplishments of the day's rehearsal. You could then ask several students to read their lists aloud at the beginning of the next rehearsal.

Helping Students Maintain Attention

You can help students who stop concentrating by involving them directly in class activity. One possibility is to name one student as a "timekeeper" whose job it is to keep the rehearsal on schedule. Outline the rehearsal plan and your anticipated time schedule on the board (or, better yet, have the students estimate the time needed for each piece to be rehearsed), and have the timekeeper check off each part of the outline as he or she observes that it has been accomplished. If you run behind schedule, move ahead to the next item when the timekeeper declares, "Time's up."

Helping Students Deal with Excess Energy

If students seem to crave excitement or activity, you could vary the dramatic energy you invest in your teaching. Use frequent modulations of vocal volume, change your physical location in the room, and employ a variety of visual and aural support materials. You could also vary the output you require from the students by giving them something physical to do. Even distributing ordinary pipe cleaners that they can manipulate with their fingers while you ask them to focus their brains on learning and singing can be helpful.

Helping Students with Low Mental Energy

You can tell that students' alertness is flagging if they yawn, stretch, appear to be trying to create discomfort in order to stay awake, concentrate inconsistently, or miss parts of the directions. Notice the physical conditions of the room. Does the window need to be opened, allowing fresh air to circulate? Have students been seated for thirty minutes with no movement? In these instances, become particularly creative with movement in the rehearsal. A quick game of "Simon Says" is often an effective way to stimulate energy in students, provided that you return immediately to the musical tasks of the rehearsal.

There are endless ways to build physical movement into a lackluster situation. You might have the odd numbered rows of students tap or snap the beat while the even numbered rows sing, switching roles every four measures. Or you could teach basic conducting patterns and have students either conduct themselves (all at once!) or a recorded piece of music related to the concepts you are teaching.

Notice carefully the effect any physical movement has on the sound produced by the singers. Strive to find motions that result in a free, vibrant vocal sound. Just as in conducting, these movements are usually fluid in nature and tend to avoid sudden, downward motions. You may find that judicial use of students' movement helps focus enough attention away from singing and toward the motion that choral tone actually improves.

Helping Students Sustain Mental Effort

Some students have trouble finishing homework or class work. They want to succeed but lack the "fuel" to sustain effort. Limit rehearsal goals for these students by working on just one phrase or page of each piece per rehearsal, keeping the pace of the rehearsal rapid and praising each accomplishment along the way. Give students frequent breaks, allowing them to stand or move around the room. While this can be effective with one or two students (use a prearranged visual signal such as raising your palm or touching a finger to your nose to indicate that you will allow the student to move and when to return), an entire classroom of students could be allowed to move about as needed. You may want to stipulate that any students who do not remain active participants in the rehearsal activities will need to return to their seats.

Gently alerting students to important information by a touch on a shoulder or by saying, "Now listen very carefully" is often effective. If a student seems disinterested, use your own knowledge of that student's affinities if at all possible: "I remember that Julie told us about riding her horse the other day. Julie, do you see any way that the rhythm of this piece might be similar to the rhythm of a horse's gait?"

Helping Students Draw on Prior Knowledge

Students who are not challenged to use their existing stores of knowledge to help them understand new information often appear bored. One way to generate interest while using the strengths and knowledge of various students is to relate a musical concept to a sports concept. For example, use imagery comparing a long, ringing note to a spiraling football pass (yes, have the quarterback in your baritone section give a quick lesson on proper form!), comparing the energy required to sing a long phrase to lap swimming, or comparing the vocal energy required for a high note to the gathering of physical inertia (momentum) required for a triple lutz jump in figure skating.

Other ways to use prior knowledge are to engage students in activities that use both memory and attentional capacities. Two ideas are presented below:

- Music Editor. Ask students, "What did the composer choose to do at this point?" "Why do you suppose she made this choice?" "Would you have chosen something different?" The ensuing discussion will encourage students to become aware of the specific musical instance and draw upon prior musical or historical knowledge to formulate their own choices.
- Music Biographer. Ask students, "What happened in the composer's life just before this was written?" When you have received the answer to the first question, ask, "How do you think this might have influenced this piece of music?"

THREE KINDS OF MEMORY

Most of us know that there are three types of memory: short term memory, active working memory, and long term memory. The following discussion describes these types and presents ideas you can use to help students remember what they have learned in class.

Short Term Memory

Information stored in short term memory lingers there very briefly. If information in short term memory is no longer considered relevant, it is discarded. If it is considered important, it is sent on to active working memory. But some students have difficulty remembering relevant information for any length of time even if they want to. These students may profit from repeating instructions and explanations back to you. Try speaking more slowly and deliberately and cut the amount of teacher verbiage in the middle of rehearsal. Some students may need to be placed close to you to reduce the frequency of their wavering attention.

Other students may have difficulty remembering the music they are trying to learn. If possible, take advantage of a student's strength in a particular modality (kinesthetic, visual, or aural). For example, incorporate Kodály hand signals or other movement into the teaching of a melodic line. Have students improvise on a given melodic fragment or theme, and then ask them for a literal repeat of the original fragment. Encourage them to mark problem spots, form, and dynamics in their music in pencil. It may be worthwhile to base a daily grade on the effective use of annotations in the score. Have students record rehearsals and practice using tapes at home. It may be useful to ask students if they have developed "memory plans" in other subject areas and if those can be adapted to preparation for choral music classes. The memory plan might include:

- a way to decide what's important (for instance, the rhythm of "Niska Banja")
- a way to help students remember the basic outline of the information presented (for instance, the form and related rhythms of "Niska Banja")
- a way to remind them that they will be held accountable for remembering.

Active Working Memory

Think about all of the pieces of information students need in order to sight-read a piece of choral music. They have to know how to hold the music, negotiate the staves, focus on their notes, remember the note they're singing, anticipate the next note, decipher rhythms, and decide what all of this has to do with a tonal center. All of that information is held in active working memory. Many students can learn to be reasonably good at doing all of these things, but perhaps you have some students for whom maintaining and using information appears to be practically impossible.

To help these students, start by trying to determine the basic difficulty. Is the student having a problem with all parts of memory, or is the trouble more isolated, such as rhythmic, melodic, textual, or vocal production?

Focus on the difficult issue while using the student's existing strengths. Encourage the use of audio recorders in the classroom and at home. Because students with insufficient active working memory skills may have trouble working rapidly, they may need to be given more time to complete assignments or smaller amounts of work to complete.

Long Term Memory

Long term memory links new information to existing knowledge in various ways, including pairing associations so that two pieces of information are stored together; categorizing information (placing information into preexisting or new groups); identifying rules and recurring patterns; and linking information (placing information in steps or a very specific serial order, each of which cues the next piece of information).

Difficulty with long term memory can be one of the most frustrating conditions a student and a teacher may struggle with. Students suffering from memory retrieval problems may work to learn a piece of music methodically or commit themselves to becoming musically literate, only to find they cannot recall what they have worked so hard to learn.

Recognizing information is easier than retrieving it. To help a student along, you might ask, "When we sang Bernstein's 'Gloria Tibi,' we noticed something about the meter signature. What is similar about the meters of 'Gloria Tibi' and 'Niska Banja'?" This approach allows students to participate in class discussions without relying exclusively on long term memory. You can also ask open-ended questions with many possible answers.

Monitor what you are asking the student to remember. Is the student being asked to remember details he or she can just as easily look up in a reference book? Is that the most important thing to concentrate on? Or could the student concentrate more effectively on notes and rhythms?

HELPING STUDENTS USE THEIR KNOWLEDGE

Even though they may have acquired information relatively easily, some students may have trouble using it. There are at least five ways in which we can observe how students use acquired information, including previewing, facilitation and inhibition, tempo control, self-monitoring, and reinforcement.

Previewing

Previewing is the ability to foresee potential outcomes. Students unable to focus on outcomes are like photographers who don't use view finders. They may be doing the work, but they have no idea what the results will be. Share rehearsal plans with these students. Tell them what they will be doing and what you anticipate the outcome will be. Ask a few "what-if" questions: "What if we practice without the piano?" "What if you stand frozen like a statue when you sing this phrase?" "What if you sing forte while the rest of your section sings piano?"

Try "composer prediction" with the students before they hear a piece for the first time. Ask them to read the text and predict, for example, what the form of the music might be (ABA, Rondo, or so on). Then diagram the form of the music on the board and add to the diagram with predictions of tempo, melodic contour, texture, and other features. This exercise can be refined further by asking the students to look at a page of new music and predict how the music will sound by noticing its expressive markings.

Facilitation and Inhibition

Capability in this area determines how desired responses or actions are facilitated and how undesirable ones are stopped. Students who lack appropriate inhibitions behave impulsively, often moving extraneously or talking spontaneously. A game of "opposing teams" may guide students toward recognizing appropriate and inappropriate behavior. Divide the choir into two sections and begin rehearsing as usual, but alternate which group sings, even on every other phrase. Another possibility is to choose a familiar piece and conduct it with unexpected expressive gestures signaling rallentandos, crescendos, and fermatas.

Tempo Control

Tempo control relates to the rate of speed and the pacing of actions. Students who work extraordinarily slowly or who rush through their work may have problems with tempo control. These students have trouble thinking through consequences and may exhibit hyperactivity. The time-keeper role described above may help a student pace him or herself. Other tempo-management activities that can provide outlets for these students include having them erase the board, distribute music, or sort music while still singing in rehearsal ("while still singing" is the most important part!), or tap the rhythm of the words on a thigh.

Self-Monitoring

You might see problems with self-monitoring in students who have difficulty detecting mistakes when singing a choral passage or who have trouble evaluating and interpreting feedback. Get these students to ask themselves, "Did Mr. Freer accomplish his goals for this rehearsal?" Tell them to be ready to describe what they think your goals were and if they were accomplished. Another effective self-monitoring exercise for students is to sing a piece or phrase into an audio recorder and then submit the recording when they are pleased with the results. A student can also take on the role of reviewer. Have him or her write a review of a video performance of a model choir from the point of view of a music reviewer employed at a newspaper. Alternatively, have students write a review of a video performance of their own choir.

Reinforcement

Some students don't or can't apply skills that they previously mastered. They need ongoing encouragement for their problem-solving efforts. ("It sounded great when we sang it last week. What made that performance successful?") While it is important to use a variety of teaching techniques, use each one consistently so that these students are given opportunities to learn similar concepts in similar ways.

INVOLVING STUDENTS WITH SPECIAL NEEDS: A FEW THOUGHTS

You may be asked to include, or mainstream, students with a variety of special needs in your choir rehearsals. With the support of your school community, this mainstreaming can usually be accomplished successfully. Before classes begin, consult your school psychologist or the relevant school support committee to determine the specific skills and challenges of those students who will be enrolled in your classes. Most importantly, keep the lines of communication open with the support staff so that you can continually participate in creating appropriate and successful learning opportunities for each of your students.

Here are some essentials that can help both you and your choirs when including students with special needs:

- Students with special needs often have aides in their classrooms. These aides should always accompany them to your rehearsals unless you specifically arrange otherwise.
- Of the professional staff assisting students with special needs, you should be the one who determines which section or choir would provide the best placement for a particular student.
- You should also be the professional who determines when a particular student is not able to function in a specific environment or situation.
- A respected, dependable student or group of students will often jump at the opportunity to work with or look out for the needs of certain individuals with special needs or abilities.
- You should ensure that the choir understands the situation and maintains pride in its supportive, caring role.

Under these circumstances, choral students can learn and grow both musically and socially through their interaction with all types of learners. The students with special needs, in turn, benefit by participating in a prestigious choir: a win/win situation!

COOPERATIVE LEARNING AND CHORAL MUSIC

Since the dawn of choral music education, choral music teachers have taught students in groups. Without groups we would not have choral ensembles to conduct. But group learning is not cooperative learning.

Cooperative learning is a planned, carefully constructed learning experience in which each participant has a role and shares responsibility for the learning. It is always the teacher's responsibility to assign students to each group. Small groups of students are given tasks, assigned roles, and made responsible for documenting their progress toward goals. A cooperative learning group usually involves three or four students, but the choral music educator may need to accommodate larger groups than would occur in a typical science or language classroom.

When groups of ten or twelve students are used, it becomes especially important that those students with assigned roles are capable of fulfilling those roles. These larger small groups also provide opportunities to link uncertain or hesitant singers with some of the stronger students in your choirs. Think carefully about where each individual student is placed so that he or she can obtain maximum benefit from the interaction with others in the group.

In a true cooperative learning venture, several distinct elements must exist: a functioning relationship among all members of the group, individual and group responsibilities, face-to-face communication, the refinement of cooperative skills, and time for group processing. Group processing usually occurs at the close of a cooperative learning experience when students are asked to identify those elements that either helped the group achieve their goals or thwarted their efforts.

COOPERATIVE LEARNING AND
SELECTED REHEARSAL STRATEGIES

Cooperative learning groups must be carefully selected to incorporate students with special abilities, personalities, learning styles, and interests. Each student should have a role in his or her organization, such as spokesperson, encourager, materials manager, scribe (responsible for writing down decisions), or timekeeper.

There are two outcomes of a cooperative learning experience: one regarding the subject matter and another involving social interaction facilitating a common goal. The group processing/reflection element is crucial so that students are able to approach the next project in a more effective manner than previously. It is perfectly acceptable for students not to have achieved their group's goal, if in the process they have internalized how to come closer to the target next time. For instance, if students are unable to achieve the goal of learning a page of music, their eventual recognition that the rhythm was correct even though pitches were incorrect will focus the group's attention on pitch issues in subsequent classes.

Planning Cooperative Learning Activities

The following discussion describes sample cooperative techniques that have been used effectively in performance ensembles at the middle school level.

Jig Saw

Although you can use this technique to accomplish many learning goals, the following description assumes that your students are learning a piece to be sung in a foreign language. Provide students with a pronunciation guide and then divide the ensemble into groups of a manageable size. Each verse or section of the text will be deciphered by at least two groups. Groups have one minute or so to elect a spokesperson, an encourager to keep everyone on task, and a checker, who alone has the authority to ask the teacher a question—as a last resort. Once the positions have been elected, the group begins to solve the pronunciation problems within a specified time limit. At the end of the time limit, each spokesperson who worked on verse one visits another group that also worked on verse one. For a shorter time period, these visiting spokespersons compare the pronunciation of the text, making note of any errors or differences of opinion. The cooperative lesson segment concludes when the spokespersons return to their home groups and share any new information regarding the pronunciation.

This lesson could be extended into further rehearsals by having the spokespersons for verse one eventually become responsible for teaching those groups who learned other verses. In this way, students with pieces of knowledge "jig saw" throughout the classroom until the entire puzzle of the pronunciation is complete.

Think-Pair-Share

Arrange your students so that strong singers are seated next to less certain singers. A brief cooperative experience might begin with the question of how to place the tongue when forming an [i] vowel at a particular point in the choral repertoire. Ask each student to think about what his or her answer might be; then the pairs of students share their opinions. A few moments of productive cacophony will ensue when students "audition" the ideas of their partners. This two- or three-minute segment can conclude with the teacher asking for volunteers to share with the choir what worked best for their pair.

Prism Concert

The objective here is for students to learn their part of a two-or-more-part choral piece. Begin by preselecting groups so that each group represents students from the same voice part, has both strong and less certain vocalists and sight-readers, and has the opportunity to use a variety of learning styles. Seat the students by groups in a circle on the floor where they may use any technique to learn their parts, as long as they do not leave their positions. You may give each group any tools that are requested, such as a keyboard, audio recording or audio recorder, bells, or other items. Or students could be just told to learn it "on their own"—without the assistance of anything other than their own voices and brains.

Monitoring the entire process could be the section leaders who have learned their parts before class. At the end of the specified time limit, all soprano groups, for example, might sing their version of the piece, one after the other. Other voice parts could follow from their various positions in the room. Section leaders could then confer to declare which groups are most correct, and then those groups might sing for the entire class. The lesson could be extended as desired by the teacher.

WHEN AND HOW TO USE THESE REHEARSAL STRATEGIES

Some traditional choral "directors" or "conductors" are critical of these teaching strategies, maintaining that the process is cumbersome and slow. Perhaps that is true, especially in the early stages. But retention of knowledge and skills can be significantly greater than retention from a teacher's commands if students have to convey their knowledge to classmates. These choral teaching strategies and techniques can be helpful when searching for the best possible ways to ensure student learning.

Chapter Eleven

Performances

The effort you've invested in your school's choral program—learning about the choirs, negotiating for budgets and equipment, planning the schedule, building a choral library, recruiting new singers, and helping students deal with their vocal development—comes to fruition during student performances that occur periodically throughout the school year. From your schooling, student teaching, or other choral experiences, you probably have basic information about how to put on performances, and there is no need to walk you through every detail step by step. However, because of the logistical complexity of large efforts involving many people, it is possible to overlook some of the fine points that can help things go smoothly to ensure a memorable concert. This chapter discusses advance planning, final rehearsals, performance anxiety (your own and your students'), and what to do after the concert is over.

ADVANCE PLANNING

The more planning ahead you do, the easier it will be to deal with unexpected events or sudden crises. Of concern to you are outside services and concert-related assistance, the availability and preparation of performance spaces, communication with parents, developing the concert programs, reminding the students about their responsibilities and activities, enlisting outside assistance, and the level of audience involvement.

Outside Services and Assistance

If you need to, hire professional musicians for accompaniment services and arrange for their payment. Ask your school secretary about the proper procedure. Get your piano tuned and run through lighting and sound cues with those involved.

Space

Reserve space for the dress rehearsal, warm-up, and performances. Determine access to concert venues for students with physical limitations. On the day of the concert, post notices stating the time that the doors will open.

Parents

Send a notice to parents stating the concert date, time, and location, the student dress code, the attendance policy, the performers' expected arrival and departure times, and the school's policies on photography and videotaping. If desired, include a statement such as: "If you bring a young child to the concert who might make more 'joyful noise' than the composer intended, please be seated toward the rear of the auditorium so that you may take your child to the lobby if necessary."

Programs

Determine the order of performance: grade level, genre, voicing, or level of musical skill. Find out if you or a secretary prepares the concert programs. In either case, prepare the information for the concert program, including a cover design unique to the performance, and get it printed or reproduced. Perhaps you could ask a student to design the program cover. Remember to include acknowledgments to the school and the district in the program. Verify the spellings of students' names and nicknames before the program is published. Very important—submit the program to your printer well in advance of the deadline!

Students' Responsibilities and Activities

Remind students about attendance requirements at the final rehearsals. Verify that they know "when," "where," and "how." Have students prepare and deliver any announcements regarding upcoming performances on the school's PA system; some students may wish to produce a "choir commercial" with recorded music or some light humor. Arrange for designing, producing, and distributing posters and flyers announcing the concert. Require that general music and other students involved include music signs and symbols in the poster design. Teach audience concert etiquette to all classes before the performance, including a discussion about how different audience behaviors are appropriate for different musical genres.

Assistance

Enlist audience greeters and ushers, or, if it seems of benefit to them, use elementary chorus members or students from general music classes. Request brief remarks from the principal and the president of the parent music organization. Arrange for chaperones for the warm-up and concert spaces and explain the logistical "flow" of the concert to them. Finally, decide how you will deal with an accident or illness occurring during the performance.

Audience

Visualize the concert from the audience's perspective. Preview the concert in your own mind and try to imagine what an audience member will experience. Will he or she experience the concert as logistically well planned and thoughtfully sequenced? Consider beginning the concert with all audience members and choristers singing the national anthem; this group sing-along gives the students a chance to sing and relax before they perform as ensembles. Plan on introducing significant pieces of music to the audience; prepare comments on musical style, text source, compositional design, or vocal challenges ahead of time. Include a piece or two at the end of the concert that uses all of the choral students singing together; this encourages audience members to remain for the entire concert.

FINAL REHEARSALS

As the big day approaches, sometimes it seems as if there are many more non-music than music activities that need attention. Issues like determining the concert dress code, figuring out who is going to go where and helping them remember, and teaching students about appropriate behavior in front of an audience all loom large, but they must be dealt with because they contribute to the quality of the performances and are crucial to your students' confidence.

Dress Code

Remind your students about the concert dress code. Decide in advance how you will handle a student arriving for a concert wearing something that does not conform to the dress code. Some teachers may not allow that student to perform; others will decide that the attendance of the student is ultimately more important than what clothing he or she wears.

Movement and Placement

Teach the students how to bow as a group. Discuss with your students whether they will applaud others while all are on stage. If students will be in the auditorium watching others perform, have them practice moving from their seats to where they will prepare to go on stage. If students are to move to different locations on the risers between songs, establish a signal for determining how and when to move. Practice walking on and off the risers.

As a mnemonic device to aid your students, try color-coding the risers and student rows. Place a small piece of colored construction paper on each step of the risers. Give the first student who will enter each row a small piece of colored paper as a visual answer to the question, "Where do I go?" Even though you will have practiced this during dress rehearsals, nervous students tend to forget logistical details when appearing before family and friends. Make certain students know where they are to proceed after exiting the stage. Determine the optimal location for you to greet parents and oversee dismissal of students. Make certain parents know where they can meet their children after the concerts. Be sure that these areas will be easily accessible despite large numbers of people.

After all preparations are made, do a complete run-through of the concert material without comment. If possible, videotape one of the final rehearsals and discuss it with your singers, noting both musical issues and performance behavior.

PERFORMANCE ANXIETY

Choral teachers (and other music educators) face a challenge that most teachers of other subjects do not: the results of their work in the classroom are presented publicly several times a year. New choral teachers may find that experience either nerve-wracking or exhilarating. If you are preparing for the first concert in your first school, you are perhaps more nervous than you'll ever be again—and it will be important for you to maintain the calm manner you expect of a professional. Fortunately, there are steps you can take that can calm both your students and yourself.

Dealing with Your Own Performance Anxiety

If your own pattern of nervousness results in becoming uncharacteristically cranky or short-tempered before a performance, give one of your more mature students a simple object to keep in his or her pocket. If the student senses that you have gone "over the edge" at any time on concert night, all he or she has to do is quietly walk up and hand the object to you. If you have trouble speaking in public, prepare a spoken welcome to the audience on note cards. Maintaining a professional posture and demeanor throughout a concert can help you project yourself as calm, focused, and in charge of the event.

Dealing with Your Students' Performance Anxiety

As you prepare to warm up your students and speak to them just before walking on stage, carefully weigh how you will use those final moments to greatest effect. Here are some suggestions:

- Speak and move slowly and calmly.
- Engage students in vocal exercises that are relaxing for both the mind and vocal tract.
- Encourage students to locate their friends and parents in the audience before they begin singing.
- Remind students that a performance is simply one step on a much longer path of musical development.

- Focus students on the fact that this concert is a celebration of accomplishments, not an amplification of inevitable weaknesses.
- If the students seem nervous after they are on stage, walk up to the risers and tell a brief joke or story. Let them know they can trust you and that you like them.

AFTER THE CONCERT

Announce the procedure for parents to reunite with their children, and then coordinate the disassembly of concert equipment. Remember that you are in charge of this event, and, depending on your contract, you may be required to remain on site until the last child leaves. Check this requirement well in advance of the concert day so that you know what to expect.

Remember to take care of yourself after the concert. Plan a post-concert dinner or gathering with friends if possible. Finding yourself alone after giving so much of yourself to others can be difficult. Take pride in talking about what went well, debrief with your peers about what didn't go so well, and laugh about the inevitable moments that were just a little kooky. Remember to reward yourself with your favorite dessert or a relaxing activity later that day.

At the first rehearsal following the concert, discuss the strengths and weaknesses of the performance with your singers. A good way to begin is to solicit comments from students in a group discussion without interjecting your own opinion. Use this discussion to establish goals for upcoming rehearsals. Later, when you are on your own, write down your personal thoughts and impressions about the performance. Make a list of items that you want to improve upon personally for the next concert.

Be sure to write handwritten thank you notes (not e-mails) to the principal, assistant principal, district superintendent, custodial staff, instrumentalists, student helpers, and parent volunteers. As a new teacher, particularly if you are heir to a somewhat moribund program, you may find that your superintendent, principal, or board members don't even show up at your concert. Don't assume they'll know what a great concert it was. Write a note describing the wonderful concert, the fine audience, and how proud they must be to be a part of a school system that supports these kinds of accomplishments. Include the program (with their names in it, of course). Thank them for their support—after all, they had the good sense to hire you—and invite them personally to your next event.

Chapter Twelve

Get Started and Keep Going

Nothing great was ever achieved without enthusiasm.

—Ralph Waldo Emerson

The first day you set foot in your new school building, you begin laying the foundation for the rest of your career. It is helpful to imagine how students will think of you and their choral experiences with you five or ten years from now. You are a role model for musicianship and adulthood. Before you get started with the academic year, take a few moments to write down some ideas about how you would like your students to remember you and their middle school musical experiences. Reread these words periodically throughout the year, remembering that you can renew your attention to these goals at any point.

Establish some traditions that will become valuable as the years progress. Perhaps you will want to create a "Wall of Fame" to record the names of students or photographs of choirs who achieve recognition for their vocal work. This Wall of Fame list can be expanded year by year with the names of other students who achieve similar successes. This is a tangible way of providing a sense of history for the students who will view these lists for years to come. You might want to frame programs and concert posters for a similar effect.

Become active in your state music educators association and with MENC members locally. Participate in choral festivals and workshops. Enjoy getting to know the professionals in your field; they can serve as your best advisors in the coming years. Involve yourself in the life of your school. Attend school events and sports activities, volunteering for as much as you can capably handle. Get to know the families of your students—they will likely be sending you more students for future choirs.

We don't really teach choral music. We teach students. And those students will grow into the adults who will sing in church, community, and professional choirs—depending on the actions we take while they are still middle school students. We must teach for understanding—for application—of musical knowledge and skills that have a place and function in the adult world. In her chapter in MENC's *Vision 2020: The Housewright Symposium on the Future of Music Education*, Judith Jellison proposed the concept of transition as a way to think about the relationship between traditional school-based music education and our goal that all people become involved in music making throughout their lives. She defined transition as "the movement of individuals across a variety of school and non-school environments throughout life" with a goal of increasing "the probability that meaningful school experiences will continue in adulthood" (p. 121). It is our responsibility to take hold of our students' abundant energy, build the opportunities into our performance programs that make the most of each student's intrinsic motivations—which hopefully include a love of music—and lead them successfully toward an adult life that sustains a range of musical interests.

Suggested Resources

BOOKS

Albrecht, S. K. (Ed.) (2003). *The choral warm-up collection: A sourcebook of 167 choral warm-ups contributed by 51 choral directors.* Van Nuys, CA: Alfred Publishing.

Anderson, L. A. (Ed.) (2002). *The foundation of artistry: An annotated bibliography of distinctive choral literature for high school mixed choirs.* Oklahoma City, OK: American Choral Directors Association.

Barham, T. (2002). *Strategies for teaching junior high & middle school male singers: Master teachers speak.* Santa Barbara, CA: Santa Barbara Music Publishing.

Buchanan, H. J., & Mehaffey, M. W. (Eds.) (2005). *Teaching music through performance in choir: Volume one.* Chicago: GIA Publications.

Carter, T. (2005). *Choral charisma: Singing with expression.* Santa Barbara, CA: Santa Barbara Music Publishing.

Cooksey, J. (1999). *Working with adolescent voices.* St. Louis, MO: Concordia.

Demorest, S. (2003). *Building choral excellence: Teaching sight-singing in the choral rehearsal.* New York: Oxford University Press.

Durrant, C. (2003). *Choral conducting: Philosophy and practice.* New York: Routledge.

Feierabend, J. (2001). *Conversational solfege.* Chicago: GIA Publications.

Fredrickson, S. (2003). *Scat singing method* [Book and compact discs]. New Orleans, LA: Scott Music Publications.

Gackle, L. (1994). Changing voice. In J. Hinkley (Ed.), *Music at the middle level: Building strong programs* (pp. 53–59). Reston, VA: MENC.

Haasemann, F., & Jordan, J. M. (1991). *Group vocal technique.* Chapel Hill, NC: Hinshaw Music.

Herrington, J., & Miller, C. (2000). *Lame brain games*. San Pedro, CA: Pavane Publishing.

Jordan, J. M. (2005). *Evoking sound, the choral warm-up: Method, procedures, planning, and core vocal exercises*. Chicago: GIA Publications.

Krueger, C. (2006). *Progressive sight singing*. New York: Oxford University Press.

Levine, M. (2002*). Educational care* (2nd ed.). Cambridge, MA: Educators Publishing Service.

Linklater, K. (1976). *Freeing the natural voice*. New York: Drama Book Publishers.

Marshall, M. (1953). *The singer's manual of English diction*. New York: Schirmer.

McGill, S., & Volk, E. (2008). *Beyond singing: Blueprint for the exceptional choral program*. Milwaukee, WI: Hal Leonard.

Neuen, D. (2003). *Empower the choir! Concepts for singers*. Waitsfield, VT: Choral Excellence, Inc. (www.choralexcellence.com)

O'Toole, P. (2003). *Shaping sound musicians: An innovative approach to teaching comprehensive musicianship through performance*. Chicago: GIA Publications.

Schmidt, S. (Ed.) (2002). *Music performed at American Choral Directors Association conventions: 1960–2000*. Oklahoma City, OK: American Choral Directors Association.

Seelig, T. (2005). *Perfect blend*. Nashville, TN: Shawnee Press.

Smith, B., & Sataloff, R. T. (2006). *Choral pedagogy* (2nd ed.). San Diego, CA: Plural Publishing.

Telfer, N. (1995). *Successful warmups: Conductors edition*. San Diego, CA: Kjos.

Thurman, L., & Welch, G. (Eds.) (2000). *Bodymind & voice: Foundations of voice education* (2nd ed.). Iowa City, IA: National Center for Voice and Speech.

Wall, J., Caldwell, R., Gavilanes, T., & Allen, S. (1990). *Diction for singers: A concise reference for English, Italian, Latin, German, French and Spanish pronunciation*. Greenbank, WA: Pacific Isle Publishing. (www.excellenceinsinging .com)

Willetts, S. (2000). *Beyond the downbeat: Choral rehearsal skills and techniques*. Nashville, TN: Abingdon Press.

AUDIO/VISUAL RESOURCES

Freer, P. K. (2005). *Success for adolescent singers: Unlocking the potential in middle school choirs* [DVD video series]. Waitsfield, VT: Choral Excellence. (www.choralexcellence.com)

Haasemann, F., & Jordan, J. M. (1989). *Group vocal technique* [Video]. Chapel Hill, NC: Hinshaw Music.

Leck, H. (2002). *The boy's changing voice: Take the high road* [Video]. Milwaukee, WI: Hal Leonard, Inc.

Levine, M. (2002). *Developing minds* [Multimedia library]. Boston: WGBH Publishing. (www.wgbh.org)

Robinson, R. L. (2006). *Creative rehearsal techniques for today's choral classroom* [DVD]. Van Nuys, CA: Alfred Publishing.

Robinson, R. L. (2006). *Jazz style and improvisation for choirs* [DVD]. Van Nuys, CA: Alfred Publishing.

Wall, J., & Caldwell, R. (1991). *Singer's voice: Vocal folds* [VHS and DVD video]. Greenbank, WA: Pacific Isle Publishing. (www.excellenceinsinging.com)

ARTICLES

Broomhead, P. (2005). Shaping expressive performance: A problem-solving approach. *Music Educators Journal, 91*(5), 63–67.

Custodero, L. A. (2002). Seeking challenge, finding skill: Flow experience and music education. *Arts Education Policy Review, 103*(3), 3–10.

Freer, P. K. (2006). Adapt, build & challenge: Three keys to effective choral rehearsals for young adolescents. *Choral Journal, 47*(5), 48–55.

Freer, P. K. (2006). Hearing the voices of adolescent boys in choral music: A self-story. *Research Studies in Music Education, 27,* 69–81.

Freer, P. K. (2007). Between research and practice: How choral music loses boys in the "middle." *Music Educators Journal, 94*(2), 28–34.

Freer, P. K. (2007). The conductor's voice: Experiencing choral music. *Choral Journal, 48*(3), 26–35.

Freer, P. K. (2007). The conductor's voice: Flow and the choral experience. *Choral Journal, 48*(2), 9–19.

Freer, P. K. (2007). The conductor's voice: Working within the choral art. *Choral Journal, 48*(4), 31–44.

Freer, P. K. (2007). Guidelines for guest conductors of honor choirs. *Music Educators Journal, 94*(1), 30–35.

Freer, P. K. (2008). Chronicling the boys' changing voice through the first century of MENC journals. *Music Educators Journal, 94*(2), 28–34.

Freer, P. K. (2008). Teacher instructional language and student experience in middle school choral rehearsals. *Music Education Research, 10*(1), 107–124.

Freer, P. K. (2009). Choral warm-ups for changing adolescent voices. *Music Educators Journal, 95*(3), 55–60.

Friddle, D. (2005). Changing bodies, changing voices: A brief survey of the literature and methods of working with adolescent changing voices. *Choral Journal, 46*(6), 32–43, 46–47.

Hook, S. (1998). Changing voice and middle school music: An interview with John Cooksey and Nancy Cox. *Choral Journal, 39*(1), 21–26.

Riveire, J. (2006). Using improvisation as a teaching strategy. *Music Educators Journal 92*(3), 40–45.

Stamer, R. A. (1999). Motivation in the choral rehearsal. *Music Educators Journal, 85*(5), 26–29.

MISCELLANEOUS RESOURCES

Feierabend, J. (2004). *Pitch exploration stories* [Storyboards]. Chicago: GIA Publications.

Haasemann, F., & Jordan, J. M. (1992). *Group vocal technique: Vocalise cards.* Chapel Hill, NC: Hinshaw Music.

About the Author

Patrick K. Freer is associate professor of choral music education at Georgia State University in Atlanta. He has been the director of choral activities at Salisbury University (MD), the education director of Young Audiences of New Jersey, and, for eleven years, taught public school music at all grade levels. Dr. Freer holds B.M. and M.M. degrees from Westminster Choir College of Rider University and an Ed.D. from Teachers College, Columbia University. He is the author of numerous resources for choral music teachers, including the critically acclaimed DVD series *Success for Adolescent Singers: Unlocking the Potential in Middle School Choirs.*

Dr. Freer is a frequent guest conductor for all-state and regional honors choruses. He has presented at numerous national and international conferences, including the national meetings of MENC and ACDA, with additional presentations in thirty-one states. Some of Dr. Freer's articles have appeared in *Music Educators Journal, Choral Journal, Music Education Research, Research Studies in Music Education, Philosophy of Music Education Review*, and the *Journal of Music Teacher Education*. Dr. Freer has served on editorial boards for the *International Journal of Music Education, Music Educators Journal*, and the *Middle Grades Research Journal.*